KINGDOM SECRETS

TO RESTORING NATIONS BACK TO GOD

KEYS TO DISCIPLING NATIONS

ABRAHAM JOHN

Kingdom Secrets to Restoring Nations Back to God
Keys to Discipling Nations

Copyright © 2017 by Abraham John

Published by Abraham John

Maximum Impact Ministries
1(800) 558 5020
email: mim@maximpact.org
www.TheKingdomnetwork.org

ISBN: 978-1-948330-38-1

Printed in the United States of America

All emphasis or additions within Scripture quotations are the author's own.

Unless otherwise indicated, all Scripture quotations are taken from the New King James Version of the Holy Bible. Copyright ©1995-2010, The Zondervan Corporation. All Rights Reserved.

Scripture quotations marked NLT are taken from the Holy Bible, New Living Translation, copyright 1996, 2004. Used by permission of Tyndale House Publishers, Inc., Wheaton, Illinois 60189. All rights reserved.

All rights reserved. No part of this book may be reproduced or transmitted in any form or by any means, electronic or mechanical-including photocopying, recording, or by any information storage and retrieval system without permission in writing from the author. Please direct your inquiries to mim@maximpact.org.

Contents

Introduction 5

Chapter 1
The Current Chaos 13

Chapter 2
The Salvation Process 31

Chapter 3
True Freedom and Power 61

Chapter 4
The Book of Acts from a Kingdom Perspective 77

Chapter 5
Administering the Kingdom of God, Part 1 99

    The King..100

    Kingdom Government....................................110

    Kingdom Territory......................................113

    Kingdom Family..118

    Kingdom Culture.......................................127

    Kingdom Decrees and Laws..............................128

Chapter 6
Administering the Kingdom of God, Part 2 129

    Kingdom Army...129

    Kingdom Education.....................................130

  Kingdom Economy...134

Chapter 7
Administering the Kingdom of God, Part 3 153
  Kingdom Business and Manufacturing 153
  Kingdom Media...159
  Kingdom Agriculture.....................................160

Chapter 8
Kingdom Evangelism, Part 1 169

Chapter 9
Kingdom Evangelism, Part 2 199

More Books & Resources 213

Introduction

"Ask of Me, and I will give You the nations for Your inheritance, and the ends of the earth for Your possession"
(Psalm 2:8).

What is happening in our world right now? What is God doing on our planet? We have been waiting for the one-world government, one-world currency, and appearance of the anti-Christ for a long time. But if you look at the nations today, there is a shift that is taking place. Nations are not trying to unite; instead they are fighting to be more independent. There are strong nationalistic movements across the globe. They want their identity and role made known and they are not willing to compromise.

In the 2016 Presidential election in the Unites States, the slogan for the winning party was *Make America Great Again*. Britain pulled out of the European Union. India is trying to declare herself a Hindu nation. And if you look at other nations you will see the same spirit working in all of them. What is going on and how should the church prepare for what is coming?

The church has been asking for the salvation of souls and for revival for a very long time, but it is now time to ask for the salvation and restoration of nations. Why nations? God is all about nations. He is either interested in restoring and impacting nations or creating a new one.

There is nothing left for God to do for us. There is no blessing in heaven with which He has not already blessed us.

- He gave us His only begotten Son (John 3:16; Romans 8:32)
- He made us His sons and daughters (John 1:12)
- He saved, redeemed and delivered us (2 Timothy 1:9; Galatians 3:13; Colossians 1:13)
- He fulfilled the righteous requirement of the law for us (Romans 8:3-4)
- He made us righteous, holy, and blameless (2 Corinthians 5:21; Colossians 1:22)
- He gave the whole earth to us to manage it for Him (Psalm 115:16; Matthew 5:5)
- He gave us His Holy Spirit (Acts 1:4)
- He blessed us with all spiritual blessings in heavenly places (Ephesians 1:3)
- He gave us His kingdom (Luke 12:32)
- He gave us the keys of His kingdom (Matthew 16:19)
- He freely gave us everything we need for life and godliness (Romans 8:32; 2 Peter 1:3)
- He gave us authority and power over all the power of the enemy (Luke 10:19)

There is nothing else He has to do for us. We keep asking for more without realizing what He has already given us and who He made us to be. The reason is we do not know how to appropriate what He has made available to us. The eyes of our understanding have been darkened and we do not see ourselves as God sees us, nor do we understand His purpose concerning our lives. We have a 'oh poor me' or 'it's all about me' mentality.

Introduction

There were people from every nation under heaven present in Jerusalem when the Holy Spirit arrived on the day of Pentecost (Acts 2:5; Genesis 17:6; 18:18). God promised Abraham,

> "As for Me, behold, My covenant is with you, and you shall be a father of many nations" (Genesis 17:4).

Then He said to him,

> "I will make you exceedingly fruitful; and I will make nations of you, and kings shall come from you" (Genesis 17:6).

He is the father of our faith.

God promised to bring nations and kings out of Abraham. We are the offspring of Abraham by faith in Jesus Christ. That is why, when the Holy Spirit came there were people in Jerusalem from every nation under heaven to witness it.

The above verse says to ask God for nations as an inheritance and the ends of the earth as a possession (Psalm 2:8). That verse is a promise to Jesus the Son of God, the ruler of all nations. Nations belongs to Him. We are supposed to ask the Father for nations to be an inheritance for Jesus and His kingdom. How that is accomplished? A study of the New Testament reveals three processes to accomplish that: *saving, discipling,* and *healing* nations.

Jesus said, "Go therefore and make disciples of all nations" (Matthew 28:19a). God is interested in discipling *all* nations. Not just one or two—but all of them. We have been trying to *evangelize* nations and saving individuals when God wants us to *disciple* nations. How do we disciple nations? God gave us the tool to disciple nations: the gospel of the kingdom. Only the gospel of the kingdom can disciple nations. The gospel of salvation will win souls. The gospel of the kingdom will win and disciple nations.

There will be nations and kings during the millennial reign. I thought all saved people from every nation will be living together as a family. That is not what the Bible says in Matthew 25:31-45 and Revelation 5:10; 17:6, 21:24-27, and 22:2. The book of Revelation talks about nations more times than any other book in the New Testament. My question is this, "Does the church currently have any plans to win nations to Christ"

Revelation 21:24 talks about salvation of the nations. There will be nations that will come to Christ. Then, in 22:2 we read about the leaves of the Tree of Life being used for the healing of the nations. God is all about *saving*, *discipling*, and *healing* nations. We are entering into a season of the salvation of nations. It's time for us to partner with God in what He wants to see accomplished.

There is much talk about discipleship, but only a very few understand what real discipleship is. Many understand the religious side of discipleship: sharing the gospel, prayer, reading the Word, worship, etc. But that is not all there is to discipleship. How did Jesus disciple the twelve? Did He have a program or a checklist of things they had to follow every day? A disciple is a learner or a student, someone who is teachable and wants to learn. Without that hunger to learn you will never be a disciple, even if you sell your house to give to a ministry. I will share more on discipleship later in the book.

Jesus said,

> "Come to Me, all *you* who labor and are heavy laden, and I will give you rest. Take My yoke upon you and learn from Me, for I am gentle and lowly in heart, and you will find rest for your souls. For My yoke *is* easy and My burden is light" (Matthew 11:28-30).

He is calling us to come to find rest for our souls and learn from Him. What does He want us to learn from Him? Who Jesus is? His lifestyle?

His values? A person can do all kinds of religious things and still not be a disciple. Jesus was not at all religious.

Hunger and thirst for wisdom is the number one sign that a person has any fear of God in his life. The Bible says,

> "The fear of the Lord *is* the beginning of wisdom" (Proverbs 9:10).

Again, if a person says he fears God and has no heart to get wisdom, the true fear of God has not entered their heart, or they are believing in the wrong god. We are all good at being religious. The world is suffering because of it.

When we restore each component of a nation, according to the Word of God (which I will share in this book), we will see nations restored to God. That is God's ultimate plan and desire. How much of it we want to realize is up to us. God has been in favor of this from the beginning of time, but man has not fully caught up with God's plan yet. God has been waiting patiently for thousands of years. The perfection of the kingdom will come only when Christ rules this earth during the millennium. Until then, we are assigned to prepare this earth as much as we can for the return of the King.

Most believers are waiting for God to burn up the earth and destroy everything, but do you know that the fire will not destroy what we do for God and His kingdom, whether natural or spiritual.

> "For we are God's fellow workers; you are God's field, *you are* God's building. According to the grace of God which was given to me, as a wise master builder I have laid the foundation, and another builds on it. But let each one take heed how he builds on it. For no other foundation can anyone lay than that which is laid, which is Jesus Christ. Now if anyone builds on this foundation *with* gold,

silver, precious stones, wood, hay, straw, each one's work will become clear; for the Day will declare it, because it will be revealed by fire; and the fire will test each one's work, of what sort it is. If anyone's work which he has built on *it* endures, he will receive a reward. If anyone's work is burned, he will suffer loss; but he himself will be saved, yet so as through fire" (1 Corinthians 3:9-15).

The work we do today for God's kingdom will not be burned up. It will remain forever. The land we possess for God's kingdom will not be destroyed, but transformed to its original state when Christ comes because we will be reigning with Him on this earth forever and ever (Revelation 22:5). As Paul said in 1 Corinthians 15:53, "The corruptible must put on incorruption and the mortal must put on immortality." Matter cannot be destroyed. It can only be changed from one form to another. At the end, the heaven and earth we see today will be changed into a new heaven and a new earth.

Both Genesis 1 and Revelation 22, the first and last chapters of the Bible, say the same thing about the purpose of man. God wants to establish His kingdom on this earth and we are created to reign. Everything we do must line up with that big picture. Otherwise, we will have a flawed theology and it will deviate us from our purpose.

"There shall be no night there: They need no lamp nor light of the sun, for the Lord God gives them light. And they shall reign forever and ever" (Revelation 22:5).

It is time for the worldwide body of Christ to rise up to show forth the praises of Him who called us out of darkness. Jesus is the Son of God and He said, "He who has seen Me has seen the Father" (John 14:9). Today, there are millions (maybe billions) of children of God on this earth who are wonderfully and uniquely made. Each one should be able to say, like Jesus said, "He who has seen me has seen the Father." Each one is created to manifest the Father in a different way. Our number one responsibility is to reveal the Father to others and to the rest of creation. That is why the Bible says, "Because as He is, so are we in this world" (1 John 4:17b). Jesus also said that just as the Father sent Him into this world so He sends us into the world (John 17:18).

One of my favorite verses in the book of Revelation is chapter 11:15. It says,

> "Then the seventh angel sounded: And there were loud voices in heaven, saying, "The kingdoms of this world have become *the kingdoms* of our Lord and of His Christ, and He shall reign forever and ever!"

The above verse says the kingdoms *of this world* have become the kingdoms of our Lord and of His Christ. It does not say, the kingdoms of the world to come, or some kingdoms of another world, but the kingdoms of this present world have become the kingdoms of our Lord Jesus Christ and He shall reign forever and ever. We have been waiting for the destruction of this world and its kingdoms. We do not even have the slightest plan of turning this world to become the kingdoms of our Lord. In this book you will find out that it is possible to bring nations to Christ in this day and age.

May the Lord use this book to accomplish that purpose.

Abraham John

Chapter 1

The Current Chaos

"The nations have sunk down in the pit which they made; in the net which they hid, their own foot is caught"
(Psalm 9:15).

Since the first century, every generation has thought and believed they were the last generation and that Jesus was going to return in their lifetime. The reason they believed that is because the signs of the end times were present in the nations of the world. The last days actually began on the Day of Pentecost! Acts 2:17 says,

> "And it shall come to pass in the last days, says God, that I will pour out My Spirit on all flesh; your sons and your daughters shall prophesy, your young men shall see visions, your old men shall dream dreams."

Peter was quoting this verse from the book of Joel and claiming that Joel's prophecy had been fulfilled.

The Chaos Is Our Fault

Because of the last day syndrome, or the rapture syndrome, the body of Christ, with just a few exceptions, never became fully engaged in what was going on in their nations. They have an 'I-am-out-of-here-any-minute' attitude and speak doom and gloom over nations and the earth, instead of speaking life. As a result, we have made many errors and brought forth chaos and destruction.

Everywhere I go, I hear believers say that this world is not going to get any better—and they've been saying that for hundreds of years. Imagine millions of people saying the same thing! There is power in our words.

Instead of speaking doom, gloom, and despair, we are supposed to be saying, "Let His will be done on earth as it is in heaven," because through Jesus Christ, God has reconciled things in heaven and things on earth. It happened more than two thousand years ago. That means there is no division between heaven and earth and God's will can be accomplished on this earth as it is in heaven. That means the situation on earth is supposed to get better.

> "And by Him to reconcile all things to Himself, by Him, whether things on earth or things in heaven, having made peace through the blood of His cross" (Colossians 1:20; Ephesians 1:10).

How is this world supposed to get any better? Did it not improve after the death and resurrection of our Lord Jesus Christ? It definitely did. He defeated the devil and sin on the cross and set all humanity free. He took the authority back from the devil and gave it to the church. We have made tremendous progress in every sphere of life; that hadn't happened since Adam walked on this earth. Now we are waiting for God to *wrap up* everything, but He is waiting for us to *catch up* with what He is doing instead. Below are some examples of the chaos we are allowing in our nation.

CHAPTER 2| THE CURRENT CHAOS

Of the 250,000 Protestant churches in America, 200,000 are either stagnant (with no growth) or declining. That includes 80% of the churches in America—and maybe the one you attend, if you attend at all.

There are less than half the numbers of churches today than there were only one hundred years ago.

- In America, 3500 – 4000 churches close their doors each year.[1]
- Half of all churches last year did not add one new member through conversion growth.[2]
- Churches lose an estimated 2,765,000 people each year to nominalism and secularism.[3]
- 1,400 pastors in America leave the ministry monthly.[4]
- Only 15% of churches in the United States are growing, and just 2.2% of those are growing by conversion growth.[5]
- 10,000 churches in America closed their doors in a five-year period.[6]
- 40-60 % of Protestant believers do not attend any church.[7]

---

1 D. J. Chuang, "Churches closing and pastors leaving," @djchuang, May 23, 2010, accessed February 10, 2017, http://djchuang.com/2010/churches-closing-and-pastors-leaving/.

2 Ibid.

3 Ibid.

4 Ibid.

5 Ibid.

6 Ibid.

7 Kelly Shattuck, "7 Startling Facts: An Up Close Look at Church Attendance in America • ChurchLeaders.com," ChurchLeaders.com, December 30, 2015, accessed February 10, 2017, http://churchleaders.com/pastors/pastor-articles/139575-7-startling-facts-an-up-close-look-at-church-attendance-in-america.html.

- About 60% of marriages end up in divorce and the second-marriage percentage for divorce is even higher.[8]
- Teen pregnancies: A million or more abortions happen every year.[9]
- Suicide is the second-leading cause of death for people ages 10-24. On an average, 117 suicides happen every day. More teenagers and young adults die from suicide than from cancer, heart disease, AIDS, birth defects, stroke, pneumonia, influenza, and chronic lung disease combined.[10]
- More than 1,500 people die each day from cancer.[11]
- In 2017, more than 94 million people were no longer in the work force. Some are baby boomers who are now retiring, but others have lost their jobs altogether.[12]
- Nearly twenty thousand people die every day because of hunger and hunger-related causes in this world. In one part of the world people die for lack of food and on the other side of the world people die because of food or food-related diseases and sicknesses.[13]

---

8 "Marriage and Divorce," Psychology Topics, American Psychological Association, accessed February 10, 2017, http://www.apa.org/topics/divorce/.

9 Abort73.com, "U. S. Abortion Statistics," Loxafamosity Ministries, accessed February 10, 2017, http://abort73.com/abortion_facts/us_abortion_statistics.

10 Erin M. Sullivan, MPH, Joseph L. Annest, PhD, Thomas R. Simon, PhD, Feijun Luo, PhD, and Linda L. Dahlberg, PhD, "Suicide Trends Among Persons Aged 10–24 Years — United States, 1994–2012," Centers for Disease Control and Prevention, March 06, 2015, accessed February 10, 2017, https://www.cdc.gov/mmwr/preview/mmwrhtml/mm6408a1.htm.

11 "Helping Families Face the Challenges of Cancer," Cancer Facts, accessed February 10, 2017, http://www.thomlatimercares.org/Cancer_Facts.htm.

12 Susan Jones, "Record 94,708,000 Americans Not in Labor Force; Participation Rate Drops in May," CNS News.com, June 03, 2016, accessed February 10, 2017, http://www.cnsnews.com/news/article/susan-jones/record-94708000-americans-not-labor-force-participation-rate-drops.

13 "Hunger and World Poverty," Poverty.com - Hunger and World Poverty, accessed

- 99.9% of people do not know the reason for their existence.[14]

All over the world people are not happy with their government and those in leadership in their nations. The national debt in the USA is approaching twenty trillion dollars. Corruption is a major problem in all walks of life. Our educational system has become bureaucratic and unwieldy; it is no longer functioning successfully. It is not sufficient to prepare our children for their future.

The majority of the problems listed above are present only in the United States. I don't have room to list all the problems in every nation. If you are reading this from another country, make a list of the problems you are facing and see if the church in your nation is prepared to solve any of them. Is the body of Christ prepared to tackle any of these problems? I doubt it. Nevertheless, the church is supposed to offer solutions because we have God, and His Holy Spirit is living inside us. We are the light of the world. Light is the solution for darkness. Spiritually speaking, if there is any work of darkness, light (the church) is supposed to be the solution.

My intention in writing this book is to provide solutions to all the problems mentioned above and more. If the body of Christ is willing to listen to what the Spirit is saying to the church and train its people to take appropriate action, I guarantee we can win any nation to Christ within ten to fifteen years. That is exciting to me! That means we can see *nations* coming to Christ in our lifetime.

Why are we facing these problems in our society? What is the root cause of them? We have been blaming all our problems on sin and Satan for a long time. I thought Jesus came to solve the problems of sin and Satan. If He solved them, then why do these problems still exist in the 21st century?

February 10, 2017, http://www.poverty.com/.

14 "6,783,907,459 in the World – How Many Know Their Purpose in Life?," Life on Purpose Institute, June 03, 2009, accessed February 10, 2017, http://www.lifeonpurpose.com/6783907459-in-the-world-how-many-know-their-purpose-in-life/.

We have more believers, pastors, miracle workers, churches, and Bible schools than any other time in the history of the church, but we do not see the same result as in the first century. Why? Did the Holy Spirit lose His power? Did Jesus Change? No. The Bible says Jesus is the same yesterday, today, and forever (Hebrews 13:8). Something happened to the message we preach. The reason we do not see the same result as the apostles is because we do not preach the same message they preached. We preach a religious gospel while they preached a kingdom gospel. Whatever message we preach we will receive the appropriate result.

In the last few centuries the main goal of our preaching has focused on getting people to heaven. We neglected the earth God gave us and we neglected the nations we are living in. In the Old Testament, when people were saved or delivered they had something to show for it. They had the spoils of war. In today's *Churchianity*, when people are saved they have nothing to show, nor do they know what they are saved from. They will say they are saved from hell. Jesus did not come to save us from hell. We were not in hell. He came to save us from our sins (Matthew 1:21; John 1:29).

The Reason for the Chaos

What is sin? Sin means to miss the mark or miss the target. What is our mark or target? These problems exist mainly because of a single reason: Humans do not know the reason for their existence. Mankind has lost its purpose. They have deviated from their purpose and they are daily plunging deeper and deeper into mire from which they cannot pull themselves out. There is only one way to solve this problem, and that is to restore mankind to their original intent. When man is restored back to his original intent, the church will function as intended and the nations will be restored to God.

When mankind is restored to this original intent, I believe 99% of the problems we are experiencing will disappear from our society and the world. Even the problems animals have, including the fish in the ocean and birds in the air, will also be solved because the troubles they have are caused by humans. When we do not know the purpose of a thing, abuse is inevitable. The reason the church is not effective in nations is because the people who are part of the church are misinformed about why God created them.

Why would I talk about the purpose of man in a book about the kingdom and the church? I heard a story about a man and his young son. One day the man came back from work and was reading the newspaper and resting. His son kept interrupting him, asking him questions and wanting his dad to play with him. His dad took a sheet of the newspaper that had a picture of the world map. He tore it into pieces and gave it to his son and asked him to go and put it all back in order, thinking that would keep him busy for a while.

To the Dad's amazement, his son came back within few minutes and the map was all put together in order. He asked, "Son, how did you do this so fast? The son said, "Dad, there was a picture of a man on the other side. I just put together the man and the world came back into order." I thought that was profound. When we discover our purpose and know why we are here, the whole world will be in order.

In any arena we look, we will see plenty of challenges and problems. These problems are there for a reason. Actually, they are not problems, but opportunities, just waiting for kingdom-minded people to solve them. Nations are ripe for harvest, and the way to harvest them is through solving their problems.

God creates opportunities and disguises them in what we tend to regard as problems. While the unbeliever may view a situation as an unsolvable problem, complaining and griping, believers are to step in, offering solutions and showing the world the wisdom and greatness of our God. Unfortunately, it's been happening the other way around and the ungodly have been coming up with solutions. This will change only when His children have a kingdom mindset. Otherwise, we will remain part of the problem or join in blaming others for it.

The Bible is a book of patterns, examples, types, and principles. They are there for us to learn and apply to our lives and situations.

In the Psalms, we read that God destroyed the provision of bread from Egypt and caused the famine to come. Then He gave the king a dream about it and hid from him its interpretation. It was a divine setup.

> "Moreover He called for a famine in the land; He destroyed all the provision of bread" (Psalm 105:16).

God Almighty called for a famine. I wonder how many things have been called or appointed by God in our nations that we completely misunderstood. I am not saying all the problems listed above are setup by God. Of course, the devil comes to steal, kill, and destroy. But even if they are caused by the devil, we are the ones who are supposed to have the solutions.

We blame the devil or wicked people for every problem. In how many nations today are people suffering because of a lack of food and various other problems? These are all divine setups for evangelizing and harvesting those nations. *Lord, please open our eyes to see, and our understanding to recognize these opportunities according to Your perspective.*

People of Restoration

Nations are waiting to be restored back to God. The land is crying out for healing.[15] All creation is groaning for its redemption and restoration.[16] Who is supposed to do this? We, the church, are supposed to do it.

> "All nations whom You have made shall come and worship before You, O Lord, and shall glorify Your name" (Psalm 86:9).

---

15 See 2 Chronicles 7:14.

16 See Romans 8:19-21.

Chapter 2 | The Current Chaos

We will not solve the problems in our nations through electing someone new to office every few years. We have been trying that for a long time. Politicians are people just like us. They are affected by the same problems. Most do not know why they became politicians so they lie, cheat, scam people, and rob their nations. If politicians could have solved a nation's problems they would have done it by now. In Egypt, Pharaoh could not solve the famine problem; it was a child of God who came up with the solution. As a matter of fact, politicians and preachers are supposed to be solving those problems but they have no idea how. We need a new breed of politicians and preachers with a different mindset and heart.

We must raise up a new breed of politicians, businessmen and women, and believers, who will go into every walk of life to rebuild the pillars and foundations of nations that have been broken down. If you are already doing this, may the Lord bless and increase you more and more.

> "If the foundations are destroyed, what can the righteous do?" (Psalm 11:3).

In the Gospels, Jesus said very little about Himself, but a whole lot about His kingdom. Why is that? When you want to travel or migrate to a country, you are not going there because you love their president. You do not move to a country by choosing which has the best-looking leader. You want to move to a country because of the benefits, convenience, security, and comfort it has to offer you and your family. That is what Jesus was offering to the people. He was offering them His kingdom. The first benefits He offered them were food, clothing, and shelter.[17]

As His people, we need to be restored to our original purpose and assignment, so that we can restore nations to God.

---

17 See Matthew 6:33.

What Is Our Original Purpose and Assignment?

Every single person who has ever lived on this earth asks the same questions: Who am I? Why am I here? Where did I come from? Unless people discover the answers to those questions, they will never be truly happy or die fulfilled.

Our God is a King. He has a kingdom. He decided to extend that kingdom to a planet called Earth. He needed someone to manage that kingdom for Him so He created a special species in His image and likeness called human beings, who are His children.

Genesis 1:26 is one of the most important verses in the Bible, one that every believer should memorize. We should teach this verse to our children first, even before we teach them John 3:16 or any other verses. This is lesson number one. If we do not understand this verse, we will miss the entire purpose of our existence on this earth. This single verse contains the intent of the Creator for creating us as a species.

> "Then God said, 'Let Us make man in Our image, according to Our likeness; let them have dominion over the fish of the sea, over the birds of the air, and over the cattle, over all the earth and over every creeping thing that creeps on the earth'" (Genesis 1:26).

God Almighty has hidden the answers to the age-old questions people have been asking in that single verse. It reveals our *identity* (who am I?). We are created in the image and likeness of God Almighty. Secondly, it reveals the *source* (where did I come from?). We come from God because He said, "Let Us create man" and He sent us here. Thirdly, *purpose* (why am I here?). We are created to have dominion on this earth.

Personalize and learn that Scripture! In the place it says, "Then God said, 'Let Us make man,' we should put our name and say, "Then God said, 'Let Us make (my source) Abraham John in Our image, according to Our likeness (my identity, I am just like my heavenly Father); let Abraham

<u>John</u> have dominion (my purpose) over the fish of the sea, over the birds of the air, and over the cattle, over all the earth and over every creeping thing that creeps on the earth.'" Try that now, inserting your own name:

> "Then God said, 'Let Us make _____ in Our image, according to Our likeness; let _____ have dominion over the fish of the sea, over the birds of the air, and over the cattle, over all the earth and over every creeping thing that creeps on the earth'" (Genesis 1:26).

Whatever God spoke to the first man is still applicable to every person today. If we are affected by the sin of the first man, then the purpose for which He created the first man is the same for all people. Nowhere in the Bible do we read that God changed His mind concerning our purpose.

When a manufacturer produces a product they come up with a statement about the purpose for that particular product. When God created man He clearly outlined His purpose for mankind. Genesis 1:26 is that purpose statement. It applies corporately to the entire human race; and it also applies to us individually. Then, each individual should exercise dominion over at least one aspect of creation; that is his or her personal purpose.

God created man to have dominion over this earth: to rule His kingdom for Him and place it under His kingship. He created us as kings on this earth. What is dominion? Dominion means to rule, to have sovereignty or control, or it can refer to a territory belonging to a sovereign or government. If we put the word *king* before *dominion* we get the word king-dom. Kingdom literally means a king's domain. Kingdoms have dominion and kings have kingdoms.

There is much debate and confusion among Christians on the subject of dominion. Many are afraid to talk about it or have never even heard it. Can you imagine being afraid to talk about the very reason God created us? Many preachers and believers are afraid to talk about the kingdom of God though that is the subject Jesus preached the most. Is there a greater deception than this? In Genesis 1:26-28 God makes very clear to us what He meant by having dominion and how to do it. He wants us to exercise dominion on three levels.

First, God wants us to rule this earth for Him. The first chapter of the Bible and the last chapter of the Bible say the same thing concerning man's purpose (Genesis 1:26; Revelation 22:5). Adam was the first king and He gave the entire earth to him (Psalm 115:16). We are created as kings and priests. After Adam, his sons are the heirs of this earth.

Second, God wants us to have dominion over the spirit world. That is why He told Adam to subdue and rule over the fish, birds, cattle, and creatures that creep on the earth. How could they be any threat to him before the fall? Why would he have to subdue them? God was preparing Adam for a possible assault from the enemy kingdom by using any of those mediums. Satan and his demons were already on this earth before Adam showed up.

Third, God wants us to have dominion over the vast resources and treasures He has put on this earth. The first commandment God gave to us is to be "fruitful" (Genesis 1:28). Man is made of three parts - spirit, soul, and body. God wants us to be fruitful in all three areas of our lives. The fruit of our body is our children and the works we do. The fruit of our spirit is our spiritual children and the list mentioned in Galatians 5:22-23. The fruit of our soul is the products and ideas we come up with our imagination, to extract and use the resources God put on this earth. If you want to know more about this please read the books *The Three Most Important Decisions of Your Life* and *Releasing Kings and Queens to their Original Intent*.

The word *human* is also a combination of two words: *humas* and *man*. *Humas* means "dirt," or "of the earth," and *man* means "a spirit." Part of man was taken from the earth and part was imparted from God Himself. We are a combination of earth and heaven, natural and spiritual at the same time. We are spirit beings living in an earthly (the dirt part), or physical, body.

When asked why God created man most Christians will respond "to worship him and/or glorify him." That is the answer resulting from traditional religious teachings. That is also the answer we have been taught since childhood. The devil deceived the church and stole what is rightfully ours. We blame Adam for what he did, but we do the same thing. We let the devil steal from us what our heavenly Father gave to us, especially this earth and its vast resources.

Who is using the majority of the resources our heavenly Father deposited in this earth? It's not His children and it's not being used to establish His kingdom. The wicked are using those resources instead. An immense amount of money from the oil wells in the Middle East is being used to support terrorist organizations. What a sad situation! In many countries, the majority of the wealth and money the government gains is swallowed up by corrupt politicians so it never reaches the people who are in need, nor is it used for the development of those nations.

We have been brainwashed by a religious spirit that has convinced us that this earth and its resources do not belong to us and we do not belong here, we are just passing through and are going to fly away soon. It has been more than two thousand years. What if we have another hundred years or more left before the rapture happens? Are we going to sit around and sing our "Kumbaya, My Lord" every Sunday morning? Lord, have mercy!

Don't we even care that the devil has stolen the wealth and resources that belong to our Father? These are part of our family inheritance, and they are being used for every wicked thing imaginable and unimaginable, while we act like paupers.

> "The heaven, *even* the heavens, *are* the Lord's; but the earth He has given to the children of men" (Psalm 115:16).

> "'The silver *is* Mine, and the gold *is* Mine,' says the Lord of hosts" (Haggai 2:8)

What if a thief came and took over and was illegally living on your father's property? Would you ignore that and let him do whatever he wanted with your inheritance? Or would you go to the authorities and start the process to evict him? In many parts of the world people take the law into their own hands when something like that happens. They feel violated and angry and then go to the authorities later. But Christians worldwide have been ignoring the devil and his abuse of our inheritance for too long. They are continually waiting for God to show up to fix things for them.

Let me tell you that God already showed up in a human body two thousand years ago, and judged the god of this world (John 12:31). That was the greatest manifestation of God on earth. He gave us the authority, power, and keys of His kingdom to undo all the works of the devil. Unfortunately, we are waiting again for God to show up in our meetings to do things for us.

The Earth Belongs to Us

Jesus said in Matthew 5:5, "Blessed *are* the meek, for they shall inherit the earth."

> "For evildoers shall be cut off; but those who wait on the Lord, they shall inherit the earth" (Psalm 37:9).

> "But the meek shall inherit the earth, and shall delight themselves in the abundance of peace" (Psalm 37:11).

> "For *those* blessed by Him shall inherit the earth, but *those* cursed by Him shall be cut off" (Psalm 37:22).

> "The righteous shall inherit the land, and dwell in it forever" (Psalm 37: 29).

> "Wait on the Lord, And keep His way, And He shall exalt you to inherit the land; When the wicked are cut off, you shall see *it*" (Psalm 37:34).

If we are waiting to go to heaven, when do those above verses be fulfilled?

God did not ask Adam to worship Him. He told him to have dominion. He is not happy with our worship if we disregard the first mandate He gave to us. The kind of worship that we know today did not start until almost a thousand years after man was created. If worship was our purpose at creation, what did those people do with their lives for those first thousand years? Instead of singing, they had dominion on this earth.

It was Cain's descendants who invented musical instruments for the first time.

> "Then Lamech took for himself two wives: the name of one *was* Adah, and the name of the second *was* Zillah. And Adah bore Jabal. He was the father of those who dwell in tents and have livestock. His brother's name *was* Jubal. He was the father of all those who play the harp and flute. And as for Zillah, she also bore Tubal-Cain, an instructor of every craftsman in bronze and iron. And the sister of Tubal-Cain *was* Naamah" (Genesis 4:19-22).

David introduced worship as we know it today. But if you study the life of David, He established a kingdom before he appointed worshipers. Of course he worshiped God personally and he was a musician, but when he sang and said, "Lord we give you all the glory, power, wealth, and riches," he actually had those things to present before God. We copy his songs without ever practicing what he did for God and have nothing valuable to present before the King. He is not looking for empty words from our mouth. He is a King and He is looking for people who will bring honor to His name, living a lifestyle of the kingdom.

God's first order is to have dominion, then to worship. We have turned it upside down. Today, we try to worship without any dominion. It is time to change.

Adam disobeyed God and sin came into this world, so God sent His Son, Jesus, to die for our sins and take us to heaven, right? That's our theology in a nutshell. But, there's something missing. What about everything Adam lost because of his disobedience? Adam fell from a particular position and was expelled from a garden called Eden, which was the kingdom of God on earth.

Did Adam fall from heaven? No. If God wanted all of us in heaven singing to Him, why then did He put us all on this earth? He should have just kept us all there. Why would He allow His only Son to endure such pain?

Created to Have Dominion

Each of us is created to have dominion over at least one area of life, maybe music, science, the arts, juggling, cooking—it could be anything. God wants each of us to be a king over something, which means to rule over something He created. He wants us to imitate Him because we are His children. If there are eight billion people on the earth, each of them is created to have dominion over at least one area of life. There will be many singers, accountants, politicians, clerks, sales associates, and so much more.

What is dominion and how does a person exercise dominion? The first step in having dominion is discovering your purpose. Dominion is not taking over businesses and governments by force. That's domination. God did not create us to dominate, but to have dominion.

There is much misunderstanding about the kingdom and dominion. Man lost his dominion because of disobedience and became a slave to his surroundings and to sin, so God decided to restore man and his dominion. That is why He sent Jesus Christ to this earth.

"And so it is written, 'The first man Adam became a living being.' The last Adam *became* a life-giving spirit" (1 Corinthians 15:45).

God send Jesus (the Last Adam) to redeem, restore, and save what the first Adam lost. In the next chapter we are going to see how that restoration process was accomplished.

Chapter 2

The Salvation Process

"Be still, and know that I am God; I will be exalted among the nations, I will be exalted in the earth!" (Psalm 46:10).

In order to restore us to His original intent, God introduced a process called salvation. The whole plan of salvation came because of the fall of Adam, right? We, through listening to a religious spirit, made salvation focused on going to heaven when people die. Salvation is much more than just making it to heaven. Most of us have prayed a prayer or gone to the altar in a meeting and accepted Jesus as our Lord, but only a few understand what really happened to them. Our salvation experience is only an inch deep and we miss the mile God wants to restore to us. Once we are saved we should begin to think and act like Adam did before he fell. Let us find out what that really means.

Five Steps to Salvation

To help us understand what salvation is all about, God uses five different words in His Word to reveal His plan about it. He divided the process of salvation into five different steps. Only when you receive the benefits of all five steps will you receive everything God has in store for you. Only then will everything we lost because of sin be restored. Each individual is at some level of this five-step process. The five steps are:

1) **Salvation/becoming born again**

2) **Deliverance**

3) **Redemption**

4) **Restoration**

5) **Transformation**

Step One: Becoming Born Again

The first step is a born-again experience. The majority of believers stop at this first experience. They are born again and then wait for the rest of their life to go to heaven because the only gospel they heard is the gospel of salvation with its focus on going to heaven and escaping hell. They have never heard and understood the gospel of the kingdom that Jesus and the disciples preached.

I came to the faith through the Pentecostal movement. The ultimate goal of Pentecostal movement is to rescue people out of hell, have them born again and filled with the Holy Spirit and speak in tongues. Once they arrive at that point they stop growing. For the rest of their life because of spiritual pride, they will behave like they are spiritually superior to everyone else, because they speak in tongues. Speaking in tongues is only the beginning of our life with the Holy Spirit, and not the end. Majority of these people don't have a clue about what they are saved from.

In order to show us what God meant through salvation, God put a shadow of it in the Old Testament as evidenced in the lives of the people of Israel. They were slaves in Egypt for hundreds of years before God moved to save or deliver them from their slavery. When we study the process and the results of their freedom from Egypt, we get an idea of what our salvation experience through Jesus Christ should be.

They were not saved to go to heaven. When they were freed from Egypt, which represented the kingdom of darkness, everything they lost was restored to them: their health, freedom, wealth, and their purpose were all restored to them. God promised them a land that flowed with milk and honey, which was their place of destiny.

Why do we need to be born again? When we were born the first time, we were created in the likeness of the first Adam who sinned and disobeyed God. There is a big difference between being in the first and Last Adam.

When we are naturally born we inherit the image and frailties of the first Adam. All of our weaknesses, sins, and failures come from him and through him. But God gave us another chance to be born again through another Adam; Jesus. The Bible calls Him the Last Adam (1 Corinthians 15:45).

When you are born again you inherit the image, qualities, and blessings of the Last Adam. We receive a new DNA for our spirit; we are adopted into a royal bloodline. That is why being born again is a very important principle. It is the beginning point, but we don't become born again just to go to heaven.

> "For whom He foreknew, He also predestined *to be* conformed to the image of His Son, that He might be the firstborn among many brethren" (Romans 8:29)

> "The Spirit Himself bears witness with our spirit that we are children of God, and if children, then heirs—heirs of God and joint heirs with Christ, if indeed we suffer with *Him*, that we may also be glorified together" (Romans 8:16-17).

We become born again to get rid of the things we inherited from the first Adam. It's our choice to remain in the first Adam or the Last Adam.

Every form of evil, sin, sickness, curses, poverty, failure, pain, and brokenness comes from the first Adam through our parents. You don't have to allow these problems to dictate your future; you have a choice.

That is why the Bible says,

> "Therefore, if anyone *is* in Christ, *he is* a new creation; old things have passed away; behold, all things have become new" (2 Corinthians 5:17).

We need to be conformed into the image of Jesus Christ. This happens through our confession. We are bone of His bone and flesh of His flesh (Ephesians 5:30).

When we were first born we became a citizen of our country. When we are born again we become a citizen of the kingdom of God. After we were born, we began to learn the language of our country saying, "mama" and "dada." After we are born again we need to learn the language of the kingdom. Everything in the kingdom works by faith and by speaking the right words. It is important that we learn to speak and live by faith and not by sight and feeling. We have been programmed by the language, culture, economy, and environment we grew up in. Once we are in the kingdom it is our responsibility to learn kingdom culture, economy, family, education, government, etc.

Step Two: Deliverance

> "He has delivered us from the power of darkness and conveyed *us* into the kingdom of the Son of His love, in whom we have redemption through His blood, the forgiveness of sins" (Colossians 1:13-14).

The second step of salvation is deliverance. After we are born again, we all need to go through some form of deliverance. None of us are exempt from any of these five steps, regardless of which country, family, or culture we grew up in. You could be born into a royal family, but you still need to go through these five steps. We all come with different strongholds and forms of oppression, dysfunction, and deception, sometimes-even possession of the enemy, in different areas of our lives.

According to the above verse, when we were born again we were delivered from the power of darkness, which is the kingdom of darkness, to the kingdom of the Son of God. This new kingdom does not work the same as the nation we grew up in. Just like any other kingdom, it has a culture, economy, government, education etc. The culture we grew up in taught us we should hate our enemies; the culture of the kingdom of God says we need to love our enemies. In the kingdom of God, most things work opposite the culture we grew up in.

It is not easy for us to change our mindset from our old culture to the kingdom culture. God incorporated a deliverance process into our journey to help us get rid of those old ways and mindsets. Either we can yield to this process willingly or we will be initiated into it by various forms of trials and temptations.

When God called Abraham in Genesis 12, He told him to get out of his country, family, and his father's house, and go to a land He was going to show him.

> "Now the Lord had said to Abram: 'Get out of your country, from your family and from your father's house, to a land that I will show you'" (Genesis 12:1).

Why did God ask Abraham to get away from those three areas before He could take him to the land He was going to show him? Those were the areas Abraham needed to be *delivered* from before he could receive what God had for him. Each area represents something specific and we need to go through that process of deliverance too.

The country represents the culture that we live in. Family represents our reputation or other people's opinions of us. And the father's house represents the traditions and experiences with which we grew up. We all need to be delivered from these three areas if we are going to see God's kingdom and receive what He has for us. Otherwise, you can be a good "worldly" Christian and go to heaven when you die—and miss everything God has for you in this life. What a waste of energy and resources that would be!

It goes along with what Jesus told Nicodemus: unless he was born again he would not *see* the kingdom of God (John 3:3). God did not promise Abraham that he was going to give him the land. First He said He was only going to show it to him.

These three areas create a "box" in which we live our lives. Normally, we do not think outside of that box. In fact, we do not even recognize that there *is* anything outside that box. Often enough, because of deception, we do not even acknowledge that we are in a box in the first place. When you are delivered you come out of that box and into a life that flows with milk and honey. It is not easy to come out of that box. Everything will try and fight to keep you in it for as long as possible. It takes revelation knowledge and deliberate action to get free.

Many precious believers hide behind their religious, cultural, or racial pride and never go through the deliverance process. As a result, we have all kinds of problems in the church like racism, the caste system, malice, hatred, envy, sickness, poverty, and curses, in addition to other works of the flesh.

If there is any area in your life that you are not able to live based on what God says in His Word, you need deliverance in that area. There are eight major areas from which every believer needs to be delivered.

We are what is written in our DNA. We look, think, and function the way our DNA is programmed. It's the *software* by which we operate our system called *life*. Originally, our DNA was coded by the Word. We thought, spoke and functioned like God on earth. It has been scientifically proven that we can de-code and reprogram our DNA. To me that's good news. Most of us carry defected DNA, which lets us think and function less than our potential and the purpose for which God created us. We carry the roots of so many sinful default settings (malfunctions, curses, habits, sicknesses) in it. Our deliverance needs to start with our DNA.

Cleanse your DNA with the blood of Jesus by speaking, and command your DNA to align with the DNA of Jesus Christ, the last Adam, through whom you are born again. Deliverance starts from the very atom from which you were created and flows into every other area of life. We do not start the deliverance process from the outside; it starts from within.

1. Pride

The first and maybe the hardest thing for us to be delivered from is pride. Pride is the biggest hindrance to us entering the kingdom of God. When Jesus announced the culture of His kingdom in Matthew 5, which we call the Sermon on the Mount or the Beatitudes, the first thing He said was, "Blessed are the poor in spirit, for theirs is the kingdom of God" (Matthew 5:3). Poor in spirit means that we are willing to admit that we need help, willing to receive help, and we are hungry for God.

In my ministry life, one of the things I found is how hard it is for people to admit that they need help, that they are broken in some ways, and that they are willing to show their real self and be authentic with themselves and others. That is the first step toward receiving deliverance.

It is common for us to say, "I am proud of this or that" or "I am jealous." We need to put that language away and learn to speak the language of the kingdom. In the kingdom we say, "I am pleased with you" or "I am happy for you." Imagine the Father looking at the Son saying, "I am proud of you" or Jesus telling Peter, "I am so proud of you, you walked on water!" Pride and jealousy originated in the heart of Lucifer and we should not give an inch in our heart for them. They will destroy us.

Why do so many wonderful Christians die without ever entering or knowing about the kingdom? The number one reason is pride. Once we are born again, the pride of our nationality, color, culture, race, and whatever else, needs to go from our heart. We need to humble ourselves as Jesus did and as the Bible says in 1 Peter 5:6; otherwise at the end we will be humbled by force.

2. Culture

Once we are born again, we become a citizen of the kingdom of heaven. Thus, we need to be delivered from the culture of the country we grew up in, with all its malfunctions and the mindset that was formed by it, and learn about the culture of heaven. We each have past experiences, abuses, pride, prejudices, and sins that left a scar or a wound on our soul, from which we need to be healed or delivered. People everywhere think their particular culture and language are better than every other culture and language. It is the pride of man that makes us feel like that and we need to be delivered from it. Once you are free from the pride of your culture, nationality, race and language, you will have the heart to completely accept people from other cultures.

Once you are freed from your culture you will still speak your language and eat the food, but you will not feel prejudiced or prideful over others. A culture is made of eight ingredients: manners, traditions, customs, food, laws, language, race, and superstitions.

Evil spirits take control of those areas in our lives and work through them, causing us to feel as if there is nothing wrong or nothing missing. The opposite is also true. Some people believe there is nothing good in them and that they are irreparable. That is also a deception. Its purpose is to keep us trapped in a lie so we will never experience the fullness of what God has promised us.

There are demonic influences in every culture on earth. What we think is normal and good many times is not normal and good in the kingdom of God. On many occasions the culture we grew up in has imposed and ingrained limitations on us and twisted our view of life, the world, and God. We are created to live in the culture of heaven, which manifested in Eden in the beginning.

When the Israelites came out of Egypt God had to create a new culture for them by giving them His laws. The laws He gave them included every aspect of life, including dietary laws, feasts, and festivals. He was training them to have a new mindset and a new way of thinking. He wanted them to completely cut ties with Egypt. It took forty years to get rid of the culture and influence of Egypt from them. That's the power of culture.

I am not saying we should go back to the Old Testament laws and regulations. If you are a believer, He already wrote His laws in your heart. Jesus revealed the culture of His kingdom in the Sermon on the Mount. Matthew chapters 5-7 are the foundation of kingdom culture.

3. Traditions

Culture forms our *way of thinking* in us, and traditions form our *way of doing thi*ngs. Many of us struggle with traditions we received from our parents and most of us don't realize it because they are normal for us. When we hear or see something outside of those traditions we tend to fight it. Once we start to live in God's kingdom we need to learn to live above all the traditions of men and be flexible and adaptable like Jesus was when He lived on earth (1 Peter 1:18).

4. Opinions of Others

We all like to hear people say good things about us. Unfortunately, there will be people speaking negative things about us too, regardless of what we do. Jesus did everything perfectly and people spoke against Him. We may not do anything perfectly on this side of heaven, plus we have the "junk" we all went through, and the enemy will use people to speak badly about us. His intention is to discourage us.

5. Religious Spirit

Even if we do not get free from other spirits, there is one spirit that we all need to be free from and that is the religious spirit. This spirit works like an umbrella over many others. If we tackle this one, many others that torment us will manifest as well. Any time you stand up and live for the kingdom of God, this spirit will oppose you. Below are symptoms of the religious spirit in operation.

1. The religious spirit will always prompt us to look for miracles. A kingdom mindset will prompt us to use God's wisdom first, which when we apply it, will bring miracles.

2. The religious spirit will tell you that revival is the solution to all our problems. The Holy Spirit will tell you the kingdom of God is the solution to all the problems we have.

3. The religious spirit will convince you that the earth and its resources do not belong to us, but to the devil and his children.

4. The religious spirit will teach you that God created man to worship Him. The Holy Spirit will tell you that God our Father created us to have dominion on the earth.

5. The religious spirit will always require a sign from heaven to believe and to prove God's credibility. The Holy Spirit will tell us that Jesus Christ is the Sign and the Wonder.

6. The religious spirit will make you passionate about a religion called Christianity. The Holy Spirit will make you passionate about Jesus and His kingdom.

7. The religious spirit will always look for an emotional experience. The Holy Spirit will help us to walk and live by faith, moment by moment.

8. The religious spirit will always oppose the kingdom of God and its teachings. The Holy Spirit was sent as the Governor of the kingdom of God.

9. The religious spirit loves the past and the future. It has nothing to offer you for the present. It is stuck in the past. Its plan is to make you a *someday* Christian and to steal from you what God has right now.

10. The religious spirit is the meanest spirit and the worst enemy to the love of God. It will cause us to be judgmental and critical of ourselves and others, and will not allow us to show any compassion, mercy, or kindness.

11. The religious spirit will create zeal in us for the Lord, but it will blind us from gaining any kind of real knowledge. It will keep us ineffective but full of a false sense of zeal. The religious spirit thrives on ignorance.

12. Religion is always heaven-focused. The kingdom is always earth-focused: to see God's kingdom come and His will be done on earth as it is in heaven.

13. Religion is focused on escaping earth and reaching heaven. The kingdom is focused on transforming the earth.

14. Religion is about populating heaven. The kingdom is about being fruitful and having dominion on earth.

15. The religious spirit will always keep you in condemnation, regret, and guilt. The Holy Spirit will always give you boldness and confidence in and toward God.

16. The religious spirit will deceive and steal every inheritance your heavenly Father has given you as His child, so that you will not be a blessing to anyone. Or, it will keep you deprived from having any resources to impact the earth.

17. The religious spirit will try to imitate almost everything the Holy Spirit does to make people feel it is the right spirit, but it is only spiritualism or emotionalism. It has nothing to do with the kingdom of God.

18. The religious spirit will either make you too spiritual and no earthly good, or too worldly with no revelation about the kingdom of God. You would be surprised to find out how many believers know very little or nothing about the kingdom of God though they have been in church for decades. It is the most important subject in the Bible.

19. The religious spirit will make you feel that you are a good Christian and doing God and yourself a great favor just because you go to church on a Sunday morning, and maybe two other meetings (probably a mid-week service and Bible study during the week days).

20. The religious spirit will deceive you and limit your salvation experience, so you think it's only about reaching heaven when you die.

21. The religious spirit will always oppose the anointing and is the strong defender and protector of human and religious traditions.

22. The religious spirit will keep you doing the same religious rituals over and over again, while expecting different results. The Holy Spirit is a Spirit of innovation and creativity, which means He seldom does the same thing twice.

23. The religious spirit thrives on fear, pride, and ignorance.

24. The religious spirit will cause you to hate the earth and its resources God gave to us. The Holy Spirit will make you a wise steward of everything God created.

25. The religious spirit will cause you to have a passion to help the poor and make you feel that is the number one priority in life,

but you won't have much to give. The Holy Spirit will tell you that helping the poor is only one of the ministries every church should have.

26. The religious spirit will try to limit our experiences with God by attaching our spirituality to buildings, particular places, or locations on this earth. The Holy Spirit is omnipresent and the whole earth belongs to Him.

27. The religious spirit is the stingiest spirit in the whole world. The Holy Spirit will always lead us to be generous.

28. The religious spirit will not let us discover our purpose instead let us waste our time on religious rituals. Holy Spirit was sent to help us discover and fulfill God's purpose.

29. The religious spirit will cause us to hate true wisdom, knowledge, and understanding. The Holy Spirit is the Spirit of wisdom, knowledge, and understanding.

30. The religious spirit focuses on the outward appearance and false holiness and humility. The Holy Spirit is the Spirit of truth and will always lead us into truth.

31. The religious spirit will cause you to believe that being poor is the sign of being humble, being stupid is wisdom, being clean is holiness, being insecure is polite, and doing the right thing will make you righteous.

32. The religious spirit will cause people to be too heavenly minded and no earthly good. They won't have a healthy balance between the spiritual and the natural. Holy Spirit will teach you that God created the heavens and the earth.

33. The religious spirit will cause you to depend on and trust in your personal achievements, merits, abilities, and works, to please God.

As a result, we become self-reliant and take pride in our accomplishments. The Bible calls it self-righteousness.

34. The religious spirit will cause us to be self-focused and self-conscious instead of God-conscious and will produce an unnatural fear of God in us, so that we become afraid of God instead of having a relationship with Him.

35. The religious spirit will cause you to feel prideful about your religious background and traditions. Holy Spirit wants to unveil and teach us something new everyday.

36. The religious spirit will limit God to a mere temporary emotional experience or ecstasy. Holy Spirit is the Spirit of faith, He wants us to live and walk by faith and not by what we feel.

Believe it or not, the religious spirit affects every single human being unless they deliberately become free from it. It will not leave you alone. Based on the above list, please do a self-evaluation and see if you are affected by the religious spirit in one way or other.

When the church becomes free from this religious spirit we will go back to our original intent again, and the church will be restored to its original glory and power. As a result, nations will be restored to God. We need to get busy with kingdom evangelism once again. May the Lord open our eyes to see the world as He sees it.

6. The Spirit of This World

> "Now we have received, not the spirit of the world, but the Spirit who is from God, that we might know the things that have been freely given to us by God" (1 Corinthians 2:12).

This spirit causes us to love the things of this world. It loves to fight for position, prominence, personal success, pleasure and material things. It will create a passion in your heart for the things of this world and blind you from receiving the true life that is in Christ Jesus.

Those who are deceived by this spirit will not receive the message of the kingdom. Their life has been stolen from them to make the god of this world richer. This spirit will let the people have so much wealth, money, and connections and they think they are being successful, but none of that wealth or influence benefits the kingdom of God.

Notice the phrase "spirit of *this* world." It's all about this world and nothing about the kingdom of God. There are many believers who think they are good Christians because they go to a church on Sunday morning. The enemy is using them as pawns.

Anything you do, or possess, that does not benefit the expansion of God's kingdom on earth, is being used by the devil to fulfill his will on earth. The sooner you understand this and make a choice the better for your life and future. Don't be pawn in the hands of the devil, thinking you are living a good life and giving a tip to God and His kingdom here and there. Do you remember what happened to the rich young ruler, and the story of the rich man and Lazarus? Don't let that happen to you.

"And when His disciples James and John saw *this,* they said, "Lord, do You want us to command fire to come down from heaven and consume them, just as Elijah did? But He turned and rebuked them, and said, "You do not know what manner of spirit you are of" (Luke 9:54-55; Mark 10:35-42).

When Jesus told the disciples that He was going to go to Jerusalem and die on the cross, one of His closest disciples, Peter, began to rebuke Him. Peter did not want Jesus to die, and was willing to fight for Him with his own life. Jesus turned and rebuked him, calling him Satan (Matthew 16:21-23; 2 Timothy 4:10).

One of Paul's ministry companions was called Demas. He traveled with him for a while but I believe that when he saw an opportunity that would benefit him personally, he left the ministry team and followed that opportunity. Paul says he loved the present world and went to Thessalonica (2 Timothy 4:10).

There are different spirits that work under the spirit of this world, and below are some of them.

a. The spirit of mammon

There are only two masters in this world, God and the spirit of mammon, which uses money to control people. You serve either God or money, depending on whose voice you obey. Money has a voice and it speaks to you. Who decides what you do or do not do, what you buy or do not buy? Is your money making that choice for you or are you making that choice as led by the Holy Spirit?

Every believer needs to be delivered from the spirit of mammon. It won't leave you alone just because you are born again or Spirit-filled. There is a process and procedures to be free from this spirit. One of the main ways God uses to set His people free from this spirit is to tell them to give away something that is precious to them. That's the way He circumcises a heart, through sacrificial obedience.

If your obedience did not require any sacrifice, then it did not cost you anything. If it does not cost you anything, it won't get registered in heaven.

b. The spirit of lust

If you have been alive for any period of time on this planet, you will understand that lust is connected to our body and flesh.

"…having escaped the corruption *that is* in the world through **lust**" (2 Peter 1:4).

There are two kinds of lust the Bible talks about: the lust of the eye and the lust of the flesh (1 John 2:16). Both are part of this world. Every temptation and sin that comes to our life, comes through one of these. One of the reasons destruction came upon the children of Israel in the wilderness was because of lust. They lusted for meat, which was the lust of the flesh. We can lust for various things: food, sex, independence, etc.

The spirit of lust is the reason and the root of all sexual sins: fornication, adultery, homosexuality, lesbianism, etc.

c. The spirit of individualism

Individualism is a term for extreme selfishness. We have been brought up to be selfish. When selfishness matures it gives birth individualism and when individualism matures it gives birth to humanism.

Imagine if people like Joseph, Moses, Esther, Jesus, and Paul cared only about their personal success. Esther would never have gone before the king if she cared only about her success. All these people had something bigger in their mind than themselves. They risked their lives for the betterment of their society and nations. People like Gandhi, Martin Luther King, and Mother Teresa cared more for others than themselves. Their lives are written in the pages of history.

One of the reasons for the epidemic of divorce in our society is individualism, or selfishness. Individualism is the attitude that believes, "I can do whatever I want, whenever I want and however I want, regardless of how it might affect or hurt me or someone else. The focus is self-gratification. That opens the door to evil.

d. The spirit of pleasure

Have you noticed that our culture is all about having fun? I was talking with a life coach and she said, "God is all about fun, right?" I asked, "Which God?" Which verse in the Bible says God is all about having fun? Not the God of the Bible, but the god of this world. He wants to keep you busy having fun so you will never discover your purpose or do anything meaningful with your life.

Paul warned that in the last days people would become lovers of pleasure rather than lovers of God.

"But know this, that in the last days perilous times will come: For men will be lovers of themselves, lovers of money, boasters, proud, blasphemers, disobedient to parents, unthankful, unholy, unloving, unforgiving, slanderers, without self-control, brutal, despisers of good, traitors, headstrong, haughty, lovers of pleasure rather than lovers of God, having a form of godliness but denying its power. And from such people turn away!" (2 Timothy 3:1-5).

There are spirits that are working behind that nature. People need to be delivered from those spirits.

7. Past Mistakes and Failures

The most unfortunate thing you could do to yourself is quit what God has called you to do because you made some mistakes. One thing I have heard from people who accomplished great things on earth is "never quit." Regardless of what has happened to you or what you did, know that there is life after that. The enemy *loves* our past mistakes. Though God *forgets* them, the devil will keep reminding us of our failures. He will never remind us of anything good we did or God did through us.

I once felt so discouraged I began to make a list of all the mistakes and failures that happened in my life. I forgot all the wonderful things God had done for me. The only thing I could focus on was my mistakes. So I took a paper and wrote them all down on both sides and I began to feel bad about myself. I thought I would never accomplish anything great in my life because of all the stupid things I had done. I fell into a black hole of despair. But I did not realize at that time that it was a trap of the enemy.

After a couple of days I went to look for that list and I could not find it. I searched and searched but I did not know what happened to it. I believe an angel came and took it away from me. If I had kept that and kept looking at it, I never would have made any progress. Thank God I never found that worthless list. The blood of Jesus washed every mistake and failure away.

As the Bible says, the righteous will fall seven times but he will rise up and walk again (Proverbs 24:16).

8. Fears and Insecurities

If there is one spirit that will try to stop you from stepping into what God has for you it is the spirit of fear. It will remind you of all your inadequacies and insecurities and steal everything you have in Christ Jesus. It will eventually steal your destiny. We need to keep reminding ourselves that God has not given us a spirit of fear but of power, love, and a sound mind (2 Timothy 1:7).

David said he sought the Lord and He delivered him from all fears (Psalm 34:4). Different people struggle with different types of fear. There are all kinds of phobias and apprehensions. Three of the main fears are fear of death, fear of failure, and fear of man. If you can be delivered from these three, there won't be room for any of the others to have a grip in your life.

We don't deliver ourselves. By faith we appropriate the deliverance Christ accomplished for us on the cross to each area of our lives. This is accomplished through various ways and methods. Some of these are prayer, fasting, counseling, love, knowledge, etc. (Matthew 17:21; Isaiah 9:6; Proverbs 11:9). There is no one-size-fits-all method in the kingdom. There are many innocent believers who have been saved, but have never been delivered. As a result, they go through life from problem to problem, from one emergency to another, wondering what is wrong with them. This is because the enemy has a hold on some area(s) of their lives and he trips them whenever they try to move forward. They never seem to get ahead in life, no matter how hard they try.

9. The Spirit of Poverty

The spirit of poverty affects every human being. If you think a lack of money is the reason you are not doing what God has called you to do, this spirit affects you. If you work for the purpose of making money instead of fulfilling your purpose, this spirit controls you. If you think money is your number one problem you are a slave to the spirit of mammon. The spirit of poverty works in different ways in different cultures. We usually think the person who is begging on the street is poor or affected by this spirit. In the West, people think they are rich because they have more and better conveniences than people in developing countries.

What I have seen percentage wise is there are more poor people in the West than in the developing nations. In developing nations, whatever a poor person has, he or she owns it. It might be a shack or a tent. In developed countries banks own almost everything people use. If they do not make payments they can end up on the street and not owning anything. Many work almost their whole life to pay off the money they borrowed from banks. You have just enough time to fulfill your purpose on this earth.

Until you are free from the spirit of poverty you will not be able to tap into the resources God has made available to you in His kingdom. You won't be able to see it or know it.

Step Three: Redemption

After we experience deliverance we need to move into the next step of redemption. *Without experiencing deliverance you cannot appropriate redemption.* Without deliverance you cannot even see what God has in store for you or what you lost because of sin. You could be saved, but all your inheritance as a child of God, your health, wealth, and emotional well-being might all be bound up by the enemy and you will not enjoy any of it in this life.

Redemption is the process of buying, or taking, back what we lost when Adam fell, a vast subject. My book *Overcoming the Spirit of Poverty* can help you in understanding all God gave us through Adam.

Jesus paid the price with His blood to redeem everything the enemy has stolen from us. We were taken captive by the enemy (through sin) and Jesus paid the price for our freedom. He bought us back and made us His own.

> "For you were bought at a price; therefore glorify God in your body and in your spirit, which are God's" (1 Corinthians 6:20).[18]

> "In Him we have redemption through His blood, the forgiveness of sins, according to the riches of His grace" (Ephesians 1:7).

> "But of Him you are in Christ Jesus, who became for us wisdom from God—and righteousness and sanctification and redemption" (1 Corinthians 1:30).

Sanctification is part of the deliverance process. One by one, you reclaim everything the enemy has stolen from you: Your land, blessings, and every other benefit you are supposed to receive from the Lord as His child. Our body will be redeemed only after we die or at the rapture.[19]

One of the names of our God is Redeemer (Job 19:25; Isaiah 54:8; 59:20).

---

18 See 1 Corinthians 7:23 and 2 Peter 2:1 also.

19 See Romans 8:23 and Ephesians 1:14 and 4:30.

Areas of Our Lives That God Redeems

He Redeems Us from the House of Bondage

"The Lord did not set His love on you nor choose you because you were more in number than any other people, for you were the least of all peoples; but because the Lord loves you, and because He would keep the oath which He swore to your fathers, the Lord has brought you out with a mighty hand, and redeemed you from the house of bondage, from the hand of Pharaoh king of Egypt" (Deuteronomy 7:7-8).

We were all sold under sin, kept captive by the enemy, and without hope in this world. God redeemed Israel from their house of bondage, which was Egypt. "House of bondage" represents our past. Jesus paid the price and redeemed our lives from bondage, sin, and the devil, and brought us out to freedom. Once we are made free we need to stay free, trusting in His grace.

He Redeems Our Lives from Adversity

"But David answered Rechab and Baanah his brother, the sons of Rimmon the Beerothite, and said to them, "*As* the Lord lives, who has redeemed my life from all adversity" (2 Samuel 4:9).

As you begin your walk with the Lord to fulfill His purpose for your life, you will realize that many difficulties will come against you. It was David who wrote the above verse and he was a man chosen by God to be king of Israel. On his way to fulfilling that call he encountered an enormous amount of adversity, much of it life threatening, but the Lord redeemed him out of them all. If you are going through any trouble right now, know that there is redemption available with God for you from that situation.

He Redeems Our Lives from Distress

"And the king took an oath and said, "*As* the Lord lives, who has redeemed my life from every distress" (2 Samuel 1:29).

Adversity causes distress. God is able to redeem us from all distress.

He Redeems Our Soul

"But God will redeem my soul from the power of the grave, For He shall receive me" (Psalm 49:15).

Though everyone's price for freedom was paid by Jesus, not everyone will receive or enjoy that freedom. It depends on the level of freedom they enjoy in their soul. As it says in 3 John 2, we will prosper and be in health as our soul prospers. Our soul needs to be redeemed and restored as it says in Psalm 23.

He Redeems Our Lives from Oppression and Violence

"He will redeem their life from oppression and violence; and precious shall be their blood in His sight" (Psalm 72:14).

The enemy will destroy us any way he can. He looks for opportunities to cause havoc in our lives, but the Lord will not let him destroy us. He redeems us from the oppressor and violence.

He Redeems Our Lives from Destruction

"Who redeems your life from destruction, who crowns you with lovingkindness and tender mercies" (Psalm 103:4).

He Redeems Us from the Hand of the Enemy

"Let the redeemed of the Lord say *so,* Whom He has redeemed from the hand of the enemy" (Psalm 107:2).

He Redeems Us from the Curse of the Law

"Christ has redeemed us from the curse of the law, having become a curse for us (for it is written, "Cursed *is* everyone who hangs on a tree") (Galatians 3:13).

Step Four: Restoration

After we appropriate the redemption we received through Jesus, we move on to the next step: restoration. Restoration is the process of restoring something to its original intent, state, and position. If someone steals your television set and you find the thief, you redeem it and bring it back into your home. If you leave it in your garage, it is redeemed but it is not restored. When it is restored, it is returned to the place in which it was originally kept.

There are many things that have been redeemed but are not restored yet. There is a lot of restoration that needs to be done in our land and in the body of Christ. God is in the process of restoration.

"Jesus answered and said to them, 'Indeed, Elijah is coming first and will restore all things'" (Matthew 17:11).

"And that He may send Jesus Christ, who was preached to you before, whom heaven must receive until the times of restoration of all things, which God has spoken by the mouth of all His holy prophets since the world began" (Acts 3:20-21).

"But this *is* a people robbed and plundered; all of them are snared in holes, and they are hidden in prison houses; they are for prey, and no one delivers; for plunder, and no one says, 'Restore!'" (Isaiah 42:22).

Acts 3:21 says there will be a time for the restoration of *all things* that have been damaged by the fall of man, but we have been waiting for the destruction of all things for so long. God does not want to *destroy* but to *restore* mankind to their original *position* and the rest of creation to its original *state*. The verse also says that God has spoken this by the mouth of *all of His holy prophets* since the world began. Note the phrase all of His holy prophets, meaning not even one spoke anything different.

What about so-called modern day prophets who have been speaking destruction and not restoration? Do you think God has sent them? I do not believe so. If God had sent them they would speak the same thing that all of His holy prophets have been speaking since the beginning of the world. It is time for us to re-align with God's plan and purpose and not waste any more of our precious time.

Here are some areas that need to be restored.

The Earth Needs to be Restored

> "Thus says the Lord: 'In an acceptable time I have heard You, and in the day of salvation I have helped You; I will preserve You and give You as a covenant to the people, to restore the earth, to cause them to inherit the desolate heritages'" (Isaiah 49:8).

I do not believe we will restore the entire earth, but at least some areas of this planet will be restored back to their original state and intent. God will do it through the body of Christ. What the church has been waiting for so long is for God to show up in one of their services and begin the restoration and transformation process. That is not the way He does things. He already showed up on the earth in Person and gave us the keys and told us what to do with them. He will not do this *in* the church; He wants to do it *through* the church. We are supposed to use what He has given us for the benefit of the planet. Amen.

Another utopian idea we have about the restoration of the earth is that when it is restored it will look like some kind of magical world. There are some spots on this earth that already look like a magical world. When the earth is restored it will be in the same state the Promised Land looked when the Israelites lived in it. When they lived in obedience to God's Word, the earth produced in its full strength and no sickness or disease of any kind came upon anyone.

It is absolutely possible in our day and time to have the same blessing upon the land we own. We need to redeem it and restore it back to God.

The Leaders of the Nations Need to be Restored

> "I will restore your judges as at the first, and your counselors as at the beginning. Afterward you shall be called the city of righteousness, the faithful city" (Isaiah 1:26).

It is sad when people who lack common sense are elected as heads of state. They have tried to redefine marriage, the first institution God established on earth. Lawmakers and leaders do not seem to understand the basic difference between male and female, or even animals and humans. They claim to be wise, but lack a healthy human conscience that can differentiate right from wrong.

Our Productivity and Years Need to be Restored

> "So I will restore to you the years that the swarming locust has eaten, the crawling locust, the consuming locust, and the chewing locust, My great army which I sent among you" (Joel 2:25).

Many of us are behind on our purpose and the timing of its fulfillment. We have been derailed and distracted. Our years and our harvest have been eaten and stolen by the enemy. Through salvation, God wants to restore them to us so we can catch up and be in line with His timing and purpose.

Our Soul Needs to be Restored

> "He restores my soul; He leads me in the paths of righteousness for His name's sake" (Psalm 23:3).

Everyone's soul needs to be restored. When we fall or scrape ourselves, our body is wounded. When we go through abuse or any kind of trauma, our soul gets wounded and it needs to be healed. Time doesn't heal all emotional wounds, just like time doesn't heal all physical wounds. Wounds require healing; and especially the wounds that we carry that no one can see, require the touch of the Great Physician.

Our Language Needs to be Restored

> "For then I will restore to the peoples a pure language, that they all may call on the name of the Lord, to serve Him with one accord" (Zephaniah 3:9).

If there is one thing that needs to be restored, it is the unity among the body of Christ. The devil knows our potential if we are united and he brings all kinds of schisms to divide us. Jesus specifically prayed for us to be one, as He is one with the Father.

This is so we will have unity in the family and in the body of Christ. There was a confusion of language with the tower of Babel. Once again, we need to enjoy clarity in our speech and language so we can maintain unity. Language does not necessarily mean a particular earthly language, but refers instead to an understanding in our communication that produces unity of heart. There is much confusion and chaos around us. When the Lord restores our language we will all speak the same thing and think the same thing, as Paul said to the church in Corinth.

> "Now I plead with you, brethren, by the name of our Lord Jesus Christ, that you all speak the same thing, and *that* there be no divisions among you, but *that* you be perfectly joined together in the same mind and in the same judgment" (1 Corinthians 1:10).

In Acts we read the phrase *one accord* several times. It means they all had the same mind, goal, and priority. The Holy Spirit worked through the early church powerfully because of that. Today, we struggle to get even two people to agree on something because our language is not restored.

Step Five: Transformation

After restoration, the final step is transformation, or glorification. Transformation begins with our mind:

> "And do not be conformed to this world, but be transformed by the renewing of your mind, that you may prove what *is* that good and acceptable and perfect will of God" (Romans 12:1).

Then it moves to our body. The more our mind is renewed, the more the life that is in our spirit will manifest in other areas of our lives.

> "But we all, with unveiled face, beholding as in a mirror the glory of the Lord, are being transformed into the same image from glory to glory, just as by the Spirit of the Lord" (2 Corinthians 3:18).

> "Moreover whom He predestined, these He also called; whom He called, these He also justified; and whom He justified, these He also glorified" (Romans 8:30).

The third stage of transformation is the renewal of our body. For most of us it will happen either at the rapture or resurrection. There were only two people who reached that level while they were alive: Enoch and Elijah. Each of us is somewhere in this five-step process. When we have gone through all these steps, then we can say we are really saved. That is what Jesus meant by salvation. I want to encourage you not to get frustrated about where you are in that process. We will not all reach perfection in this life, though some may reach it, but as long as we make progress daily, we are on the right track and we have a reason to rejoice. Don't get stuck or give up in frustration.

That is why Paul encouraged the believers in Philippi to work out their own salvation, instead of just saying they were saved. We have to work it out to receive its benefits. It is interesting how he says, "work out your own salvation," not someone else's.

> "Therefore, my beloved, as you have always obeyed, not as in my presence only, but now much more in my absence, work out your own salvation with fear and trembling" (Philippians 2:12).

Jesus put the fivefold ministry gifts (apostles, prophets, evangelists, pastors, and teachers) in the church to help us appropriate everything God has made available through Christ. Once we are trained or equipped each of us will become a perfect man.

> "Till we all come to the unity of the faith and of the knowledge of the Son of God, to a perfect man, to the measure of the stature of the fullness of Christ" (Ephesians 4:13).

The above verse says *we all* come to the unity of faith. It is talking about the entire body of Christ, and of the knowledge of the Son of God, to a perfect man. The fivefold ministry gifts are supposed to bring the knowledge of the Son of God that produces the unity of faith in the church, so that we become a perfect man. So far what most fivefold ministry gifts have been trying to do is create revival.

Who is a perfect man? There were only two perfect men that lived on this earth, Adam before the fall and Jesus. Adam was perfect to an extent before he committed sin, but we do not have any history of how he lived or what he did before the fall so we do not have an example to follow. To give us an example of how we should live once we are saved God sent another Adam to this earth, Jesus Christ, who is called the Last Adam (1 Corinthians 15:45).

When we become perfect we live up to the measure of the stature of the fullness of Christ. What is the measure of the stature of the fullness of Christ? Who is Christ in His fullness or in His originality? Christ is the Creator and He is the King. Once we are restored we are supposed to live like the original Adam, or Jesus Christ, the Last Adam, as kings and creators. The above verse is talking about something that needs to happen down here on earth and not in heaven.

Chapter 3

True Freedom and Power

"God reigns over the nations; God sits on His holy throne"
(Psalm 47:8).

Jesus gave His disciples three things before He gave them the spiritual authority to heal sickness and cast out demons. We had lost these three things when Adam fell.

> "From that time Jesus began to preach and to say, 'Repent, for the kingdom of heaven is at hand.' And Jesus, walking by the Sea of Galilee, saw two brothers, Simon called Peter, and Andrew his brother, casting a net into the sea; for they were fishermen. Then He said to them, 'Follow Me, and I will make you fishers of men.' They immediately left *their* nets and followed Him. Going on from there, He saw two other brothers, James *the son* of Zebedee, and John his brother, in the boat with Zebedee their father, mending their nets. He called them, and immediately they left the boat and their father, and followed Him" (Matthew 4:17-22).

Jesus Offered Them a Kingdom

Jesus offered them a kingdom first.[20] Why? He knew that man cannot live without a kingdom and that is what we lost when Adam fell. He also told us to seek it first. The prerequisite to receiving that kingdom was to repent. We have been taught that we need to repent so that we can become a Christian and then die and go to heaven. But the real reason Jesus told the people to repent was to prepare for a kingdom that was about to arrive on this earth. Going to heaven or a church was not part of the reason He told them to repent.

To repent means to change the way we think. He was saying a new kingdom is about to arrive here, but that kingdom and its culture (way of thinking) is different from the nation and culture you are living in right now. In order to enter that kingdom and benefit from it, you need to repent. We need to adopt a new way of thinking according to the culture of this new kingdom to enter and benefit from it.

Following Jesus

Then He told them

> "Follow Me, and I will make you fishers of men"
> (Matthew 4:19).

For a long time, with our religious mindset we interpreted this verse as, "Follow Me and I will make you ministers, evangelists, or even preachers, so that you can win souls for Jesus." If Jesus meant any of those things He would have said that. We assume things Jesus never said or intended because that is the way we have been conditioned by a religious spirit. He said, "Follow Me, and I will make you fishers of men." What did He really mean by that?

---

20 See Matthew 4:17.

Even today, in many parts of the world people are taught that to follow Jesus means to be in ministry. With their religious judgment, they make others feel that if you are not in full-time ministry, you are not really spiritual or serving God. They believe it is only those who are in full-time ministry who really accomplish God's purposes on earth.

The Law of Dominion

What made the disciples follow Jesus? He had no mansion, no estate, no donkeys, no horses, and no servants, not even a place to lay His head. We have no record of Jesus owning anything, but people who were business owners left their businesses and their parents to follow Him. Why?

It was because He had dominion. Though Jesus owned nothing in the natural, He had dominion. In truth, He owned everything. How can a person own nothing but at the same time own everything? Through the principle or law of dominion. Though Jesus owned nothing He never lacked anything. That is deep enough for us to meditate on for a while.

The apostle Paul lived according to the same law Jesus lived. Listen to his testimony.

> "By honor and dishonor, by evil report and good report; as deceivers, and *yet* true; as unknown, and *yet* well known; as dying, and behold we live; as chastened, and *yet* not killed; as sorrowful, yet always rejoicing; as poor, yet making many rich; as having nothing, and *yet* possessing all things" (2 Corinthians 6:8-10).

How can a person who is poor make many rich and have nothing but possess everything? It happens through living by the law of dominion. What is the law of dominion? Everything God created is intended to have dominion over something. The birds are created to have dominion over the air. The fish are created to have dominion over the water. The trees are created to have dominion over the land, and animals over the forest. And man was created to have dominion over everything God created.

When you operate and live by the law of dominion, everything is at your disposal. You may not own or possess anything in the natural, but you will never have any lack; all your needs will be met. Only a very few people ever reach this level because most are trying to get more things in the natural, and trusting in the natural. Elijah, Elisha, Jesus, and Paul are examples of people who lived according to the law of dominion.

Isn't it sad that we have a problem with the idea of dominion? The birds and fish understand this better than most believers. If we could talk to other creatures, they would tell us about our purpose. Some people say we have to wait until the second coming of Christ to have dominion. Tell that to a fish, "Fish, you have to wait until Jesus comes back to have dominion in the water." It would reply, "Oh, I'm sorry. I did not know that, but it's too late now. I've been taking dominion here for a long time now. I thought I was created for it." Tell a bird it cannot fly and take dominion over the air because Jesus did not come back yet. What would be its reply? It's time for us to wake up! (Romans 13:11).

If you tell an unbeliever about dominion, they do not have any problem understanding it because they are already doing it in every sphere of life. It's in the gene of every human being—except Spirit-filled believers, it seems. What a horrible deception! If we are not living a life of dominion we are not even living up to the standard of an animal. There is nothing worse than that.

In Luke 5 we find the background of when Jesus called these disciples to His mission. He found them tired and hopeless. The night before He showed up, they tried to catch fish and could not catch anything. They were getting ready to go home to rest.

The first thing Jesus taught His disciples was to exercise the law of dominion to meet their personal needs. If we cannot meet our own need by trusting in God how shall we believe for God to meet the needs of others? Anyone who follows Jesus must begin where Adam and the disciples began by exercising the law of dominion.

Jesus blessed them with the biggest catch of fish of their lifetime through a test of obedience. They saw in Jesus something they had seen in no other human being until that moment. Though He did not own anything in His own name in the natural He could have anything He wanted at any time. Fish and nature obeyed Him. He was not influenced by circumstances; instead He had power over them. He was not under anything or shaken by anything that was happening around Him.

We calculate our blessings by how many possessions we have, how big our house is, or what brand of car we drive. At the same time, we have no dominion. People don't even know why they exist on this earth but they have all these gadgets. They are in a race to get more stuff; but the more they have, the less they are satisfied. This is not the life Jesus intended for us.

Jesus Offered Them Real Freedom

When Jesus called His disciples He said, "Follow Me, and I will make you fishers of men." What does that mean? I did not understand what Jesus meant by it and why the disciples immediately left their businesses and fathers and followed Him. I thought it meant Jesus was going to make them evangelists to go and make converts: Make them ministers and soul winners, right? Has anyone else ever thought like that?

Don't you think they should have at least talked it over with their wives or their fathers before leaving the businesses that provided their livelihood? Should they have at least found a substitute to help their fathers with the business? The Bible says that as soon as Jesus called them, they immediately left everything and followed Him! They did not bother with those things because they found what they had been waiting for all their lives. They did not want to miss it for anything else.

Peter and Andrew were fishermen. They went for fishing at night. I have seen this almost every time I go to India because I live close to the ocean. Around six o'clock in the evening, there's an exodus of fishing boats going into the deep waters of the ocean. They come back the following morning after fishing all night. Though they are in business, their survival depends on whether or not they catch any fish.

Jesus offered them something they had waited for all their lives. Jesus offered them two other things next to a kingdom that every human heart longs for. Everyone reading this also longs for these two things.

What are the two things Jesus offered them? They are *freedom* and *power*. These fall in the category of the most misused and misunderstood words, along with the word *love*.

Why freedom? They were tired of the fishing business. They had worked all night without catching anything. They had no control over their life, circumstances, or the fish. If the fish got into their net, they had some income; and if not, they went hungry. They did not get any breaks; they had no freedom to do the things they wanted to do in their hearts. If you have not slept all night, what do you do during the daytime? You sleep. But if you have a family with children, there is no guarantee that you will get much sleep. In their hearts they knew they were created for something better and greater, but they couldn't leave their businesses because their livelihood depended on it.

Millions, maybe billions, of people on this earth are in this category. They are doing something they don't like, but because they have no other choice, they continue to do what they are doing for survival. If they quit what they are doing, they will sink. They are between a rock and a hard place, crying out in their hearts for freedom and power.

Many who work a nine-to-five job are in this category. They know in their hearts, they are not doing what they were created to do, but they are not free to change that. The hope they had in their hearts for their lives and what they actually do does not match up.

Finding Real Freedom

What is real freedom? Real freedom is the ability to fulfill your purpose. Even if you live in a free society, if you are not free to fulfill your purpose,

Chapter 3 | True Freedom and Power

you are not really free. Conversely, you could live in the most oppressed nation on earth, but be free inside to fulfill your purpose. That is true freedom. Jesus said whom the Son (not the culture or the government) sets free is free indeed. Until we find freedom in Jesus, we are not truly free.

Many confuse freedom with independence. To be independent means to not want to submit, depend, or be accountable to anyone. This tendency comes from a rebellious and prideful heart. "I am going to do what I want, when I want, the way I want, and I don't care how it is going to affect others." That's pure evil, not freedom. Jesus was the freest Person in the universe, but He did not have a problem submitting to His Father, even in the minutest details. How is that possible? The sign of *true freedom is absolute submission by one's choice.*

The disciples noticed this man Jesus was different from others. They did not care if He had a mansion or a donkey. They noticed He was free and that He had power. He had dominion. Below are the signs of a free spirit:

1. Only a free person can choose to submit: Though Jesus was free, He chose to submit to His Father in everything, even to His death. Many times we confuse freedom with independence but they are opposite.

2. You are free to let go of what is familiar to you: The Bible says Jesus left the form and being equal with God and took the form of a servant, and made Himself of no reputation (Philippians 2:6-7).

3. You are free to fulfill your purpose: The sign of true freedom is that you are free to fulfill your God-given purpose. Until then you are not truly free, regardless of the culture and government you live in. Jesus fulfilled His purpose though He was born under the oppressing rule of Rome.

4. You are free to take a risk: This is another sign of true freedom. You need to be emotionally free to take a risk for God. Jesus' life story is all about taking risks.

5. You possess self-control: Only free people are able to control themselves; their passions, flesh, and circumstances. You must be free to be led by your spirit. Those who are led by the Spirit are the children of God.

6. You have the fruit of the Spirit manifesting through you: Activating the fruit of the Spirit is a choice. It is in us. You and I can choose to be joyful and choose to love, etc.

7. You have a very active relationship with your Heavenly Father: Everything Jesus did was what He saw His Father doing, and He spoke only what He heard His Father speak.

8. You are quick to repent and forgive: Jesus did not have to repent of anything, but He was quick to forgive. He still is.

9. You are open to learn new things and ways.

Jesus Offered Them Real Power

Real power is the ability to influence others and to influence your circumstances. Jesus did not offer the disciples salvation. He did not say, "Follow Me, and I will take you to heaven." No. Neither did He say, "Follow Me, and I will teach you how to conduct revival meetings." No!

Most of our evangelism has involved scaring people out of hell. I remember approaching people, and asking, "If you die today, do you know if you are going to heaven or hell?" Some people were scared of going to hell and to avoid it at any cost, accepted Jesus. But they have no idea what Jesus really offered them. We do not see such evangelism anywhere in the Bible.

I am not denying there is a hell, but hell was not the motivating factor Jesus used to cause people to love or follow Him. Not even to the rich young ruler. When He walked away from Him, Jesus did not say, "By the way, if you don't come back I will send you to hell." If someone is going to hell, it is not because God is sending them there. It's their own choice that takes them there.[21]

Everyone Wants Freedom and Power

Every human soul is hungering for these two things. What motivates a person who works from nine to five to leave work and to start a business? Freedom.

What makes a son or daughter feel like they can't wait to be an adult and leave home? What is their motivation? Freedom. Unfortunately many leave home for the wrong reasons and do not really understand true freedom and power.

Why do most people want to be in politics? For power. Why do people aspire to make a lot of money? They think money will give them power. Not necessarily.

Power is not domination or manipulating others through fear. They are wrong kinds of power. Hitler had power and influence, but it was a negative influence produced by fear.

There is only one Person who can give true freedom and power to people and that is Jesus Christ. If we are going to restore this nation back to God, we need to understand what Jesus is offering to people, and we should offer them the same. If we are going to win people to God, we must offer them what He is offering them: a kingdom, freedom, and power. We should stop offering people religion.

Do you think people will listen to you if you offer them the three things Jesus offered His disciples: a kingdom, freedom, and power? They would have to be out of their mind to turn down such a deal. That is why the Bible says in Luke 16:16,

---

21 See John 3:19-21.

> "The law and the prophets *were* until John. Since that time the kingdom of God has been preached, and everyone is pressing into it."

If you promise heaven, not very many people are interested. Come to church? For what? They will say, "You have the same problems I do. Why I should I come to your church?" Jesus did not call people to come to church. He offered them a kingdom, freedom, and power. *And they ran to get into His kingdom.*

What freedom did Jesus offer Peter and Andrew? Freedom from their job; their mundane task of catching fish every night to survive, which prevented them from fulfilling their purpose. What kind of power did He offer? The power to influence men. He made them fishers of men. Every person likes to have influence and followers, which is why social media is so popular. Influence. How many followers and likes do you get? How many friends do you have on your sites?

All of life revolves around these two words: Freedom and power. People do crazy things to have freedom and power. Why do men and women prostitute their bodies? Why do people forget all else in pursuit of money? Why do they do anything for fame? For freedom and power by their own definition.

Why do nations fight against each other? For freedom and power. Why do terrorist groups like ISIS exist? They are looking for freedom and power, but they misunderstand true freedom and power.

Freedom allows us to fulfill our purpose. You are not truly free until you are free to fulfill your purpose. When the Israelites were in slavery in Egypt they were not free to fulfill their purpose. They had to do what their taskmasters told them to do. They had no control over any area of their life because Pharaoh and his taskmasters regulated everything.

They had no power or influence in anything. What we need to offer people is not tongues. We need to offer what people are looking for:

Dominion. If we are going to finish the task Jesus gave us, a new breed of believers and ministers must rise up in this nation and this world.

First, Jesus offered them His kingdom and righteousness. Then He offered them freedom and power. Who would say no to such a grand offer? People will run to Jesus. The majority of the people on the earth are not free, nor do they have any power. Why do men and women show their half-naked bodies in advertisements and music videos? They do it for some sort of power and influence. What do rock stars and gangsters want? Freedom and power. What did Jesus offer the sick man at the pool of Bethesda? Freedom from the slavery of infirmity, which had ruled him for thirty-eight years.

What did Jesus offer Zacchaeus, the tax collector? He was not doing what he was doing because he felt stealing was his primary purpose. As soon as he found freedom, he repented and said he would give back everything he gained illegally. He discovered true freedom and true power. Why do people lie, kill, and cheat? All for the sake of freedom and power, but they are seeking them the wrong way. They will never discover true freedom and power that way.

You do everything in your life to satisfy your innate desire for a kingdom, freedom, or power. For example, a nice place to live, which is our spirit's hunger for the lost kingdom, These three things undergird our lives, whether we understand the real reason we seek them or not.

The church was hijacked by a religious spirit a long time ago and most believers don't recognize it. We don't offer people what Jesus offered. We offer a religion called Christianity or a religious experience, or some rituals. That is why more people are turning away from church than coming to church.

When you discover your purpose and fulfill it, you will automatically have influence.

The Old and the New Are the Same!

If you read history you will find out that for a long time people thought the sun orbited around the earth, and everyone believed it to be true until Copernicus began to question it. He studied the planets and how they functioned. He discovered that Earth rotates a thousand miles per hour.[22] People called him crazy.

Dear brethren, let me tell you with a painful heart that the church we see today did not exist in the New Testament. We have been taught to focus on rapture and revival and we have been waiting for them while most of the world around us is going to hell.

Jesus offered the same thing God offered Adam in the book of Genesis. He did not say anything different than what God told Adam in the beginning. He had the same message and offered His disciples the opportunity to take what He offered them. Scripture outlines this clearly:

Genesis Chapters 1-3	New Testament
God created man in His image and likeness. (See Genesis 1:26)	When we are born again, we are recreated in the image and likeness of God. (See John 3:3 and Colossians 3:10)
God blessed them and told them to be fruitful. (See Genesis 1:28)	Jesus blessed us and told us to bear fruit. (See Matthew 5:3-9 and John 15:16)
God told man to subdue and take dominion over every creature He had made. (See Genesis 1:28)	Jesus told us to tread on serpents and scorpions and over all the power of the enemy. (See Luke 10:19)

---

22 EarthSky staff, "Why can't we feel Earth's spin?" EarthSky, February 5, 2017, accessed February 15, 2017, http://earthsky.org/earth/why-cant-we-feel-earths-spin.

God gave Adam the earth as his inheritance.	Jesus said the meek shall inherit the earth (See Matthew 5:5)
God put man in His kingdom, the garden.	Jesus came to restore and give us the kingdom. (See Luke 12:32 and 22:29)
There was no sickness or curse in the garden.	Jesus came to die for our sickness and curse and gave us authority over all manner of sickness and disease. (See Matthew 8:16 and 10:1)
God breathed into him His Spirit. (See Genesis 2:7)	Jesus breathed His Spirit on the disciples. (See John 20:22)
God gave them His Word. (See Genesis 2:16-17)	Jesus gave us His Word. (See John 17:8)
They were clothed with God's glory. (See Genesis 2:25)	Jesus said that He gave us His glory. (See John 17:22)
God instituted marriage. (See Genesis 2:22-24)	When Jesus referred to marriage He referred to the original marriage. (See Matthew 19:4,8)
God walked with man. (See Genesis 3:8)	Jesus walked with us and dwelt among us. (See John 1:14)
Adam had unlimited knowledge and wisdom. (See Genesis 2:19-20)	Jesus possesses the treasures of all wisdom and knowledge and He lives inside of us. (See Colossians 2:3)

Man had dominion over the earth. (See Genesis 1:26)	Jesus said all authority in heaven and on earth was given to Him. In turn, He gave that authority to us. He said whatever we loose (or permit) on earth will be loosed (permitted) in heaven; and whatever we bind (or forbid) on earth will be bound (forbidden) in heaven (See Matthew 16:19 and Ephesians 1:22)
God told Adam everything in the garden was freely his.	Jesus said freely you have received, freely give. (See Matthew 10:8; Romans 8:32; and 1 Corinthians 2:12)
God gave Adam a woman.	The church is pictured as a woman
Adam was the son of God. (See Luke 3:38)	Whoever believes in Jesus becomes a child of God. (See John 1:12)
Genesis starts with, "In the beginning…" (See Genesis 1:1)	The gospel of John starts with, "In the beginning…" (See John 1:1)
God's will was done on earth as it was in heaven. There was no curse, sickness, poverty, or death in the garden.	Jesus taught us to pray the same. (See Matthew 6:10)
God did not ask Adam and Eve to sing to Him.	Jesus never asked anyone to sing to Him.

A river came out of Eden, parted into the four corners of the earth. (See Genesis 2:10-14)	Jesus said the rivers of living water will flow out of us to the uttermost parts of the earth. (See John 7:38 and Acts 1:8)
God told them to multiply and fill the earth. (See Genesis 1:28)	Jesus said to go and make disciples of all nations. (See Matthew 28:19)

Jesus' life and mission was a fulfillment of God's original plan we read in Genesis 1-3. My book *The Three Most Important Decisions of Your Life* covers more on regaining our original purpose and would aid you greatly in uprooting the religious spirit from your heart.

Restoring Dominion

If you study the Gospels in detail, everything Jesus did, and trained the disciples to do, served to restore the dominion they lost. He started with their personal lives. That is true discipleship.

When they encountered the storm at sea, what did Jesus say when the disciples woke Him up? He did not say, "Oh my, next time you should wake Me up a little earlier, this thing can only be handled by a person like Me." No, He asked why they woke Him and told them they had little faith. He meant they were supposed to handle the situation in a different way. He was telling them to exercise their dominion over nature (Psalm 8:6).

How much influence do you think the church has over what is going on in our nation, or in any nation? Not much. Why? Because we don't have any power. Why don't we have any power? Because we do not understand our purpose. Dominion reveals your purpose, purpose give you freedom, and freedom gives you power. Only free people can handle real power. Otherwise, power will corrupt them. Jesus asked the disciples to follow Him; and after He set them free, He gave them power to cast out demons and to heal the sick.

Chapter 4

The Book of Acts from a Kingdom Perspective

"He will subdue the peoples under us, and the nations under our feet" (Psalm 47:3).

The book of Acts begins and ends with the kingdom message (Acts 1:3; 28:30-31).

The number twelve is the number of government in the Bible. We see in Acts chapter 1 after Judas committed suicide the eleven disciples came together to select a new disciple to replace him. They gathered in the Upper Room and there were one hundred and twenty people waiting and praying. One hundred and twenty is ten times twelve. And on the day of Pentecost three thousand souls were saved after Peter preached the inaugural message of the church. Three thousand is two hundred and fifty times twelve.

Peter preached the kingdom of God

What I did not understand for a long time was the message Peter preached on the day of Pentecost. I wondered why he did not mention anything about the kingdom of God in his message. Why was it only about repentance and baptism? I was ignorant and blinded by the religious spirit for a long time and that is why I did not see anything about God's kingdom in his message. To be honest, Peter spoke about repentance and baptism only after people asked him what they should do, after they heard his preaching. The entire message he preached prior to that was about David and his throne and how God raised Jesus to sit on that throne. He preached the kingdom of God from a historical perspective, and how Jesus is the fulfillment of the prophecies and promises God gave to David about his throne.

Peter preached more about the kingdom of God in that one message than anyone else in the entire book of Acts. He referred to David and his throne several times. What does David have to do with the day of Pentecost? Or the arrival of the Holy Spirit? Or the inauguration of the church? Why would Peter refer to David in the first message ever preached in the church age? This gets very interesting. There are ten references to David and nine references to Abraham in the book of Acts.

Remember, Jesus is the Son of David, the legal heir to his throne. God promised David an eternal throne and a kingdom.

> """When your days are fulfilled and you rest with your fathers, I will set up your seed after you, who will come from your body, and I will establish his kingdom. He shall build a house for My name, and I will establish the throne of his kingdom forever. I will be his Father, and he shall be My son. If he commits iniquity, I will chasten him with the rod of men and with the blows of the sons of men. But My mercy shall not depart from him, as I took *it* from Saul, whom I removed from before you. And your house and your kingdom shall be established forever before you. Your throne shall be established forever"""' (2 Samuel 7:12-16).

Chapter 4 | The Book of Acts from a Kingdom Perspective

The above prophecy and covenant was fulfilled in Jesus at His coming.

> "And behold, you will conceive in your womb and bring forth a Son, and shall call His name Jesus. He will be great, and will be called the Son of the Highest; and the Lord God will give Him the throne of His father David. And He will reign over the house of Jacob forever, and of His kingdom there will be no end" (Luke 1:31-33).

Throughout the Gospels Jesus is called the Son of David. In fact the New Testament begins with this statement, "The book of the genealogy of Jesus Christ, the Son of David, the Son of Abraham" (Matthew 1:1). The Holy Spirit gave Peter a revelation about that when He stood up to preach. It had everything to do with God's eternal kingdom.

When those Jewish people heard that message, they were cut to the heart and ran to him. Jesus said that from the day of John the Baptist, the kingdom of God was being preached and everyone was pressing into it. Three thousand people ran to Peter to get into the kingdom that day.

> ""Men *and* brethren, let *me* speak freely to you of the patriarch David, that he is both dead and buried, and his tomb is with us to this day. Therefore, being a prophet, and knowing that God had sworn with an oath to him that of the fruit of his body, according to the flesh, He would raise up the Christ to sit on his throne, he, foreseeing this, spoke concerning the resurrection of the Christ, that His soul was not left in Hades, nor did His flesh see corruption. This Jesus God has raised up, of which we are all witnesses. Therefore being exalted to the right hand of God, and having received from the Father the promise of the Holy Spirit, He poured out this which you now see and hear.
>
> "For David did not ascend into the heavens, but he says himself:
>
> 'The Lord said to my Lord,
> "Sit at My right hand,

Till I make Your enemies Your footstool"'"" (Acts 2:29-35).

It is interesting to look at how each of the gospels presents the entry of Jesus into Jerusalem too. When the people shouted hosanna in the highest or hosanna to the Son of David, Mark recorded it with David's kingdom, which we do not see in the other gospels.

> "Then those who went before and those who followed cried out, saying:
>
> 'Hosanna!
> Blessed *is* He who comes in the name of the Lord!
> Blessed *is* the kingdom of our father David
> That comes in the name of the Lord!
> Hosanna in the highest!'" (Mark 11:9-10).

In His triumphal or royal entry into Jerusalem, He was also fulfilling one of the major prophecies in the Old Testament because He actually was their King.

> "Rejoice greatly, O daughter of Zion! Shout, O daughter of Jerusalem! Behold, your King is coming to you; He *is* just and having salvation, Lowly and riding on a donkey, A colt, the foal of a donkey" (Zechariah 9:9).

If you would like to know more about David and how he is connected to the kingdom of God, please read my book *7 Dimensions and Operations of the Kingdom of God*. Clearly God did not "insert" the church into His original plan; the church had been part of His plan all along.

Philip preached the kingdom of God to the people of Samaria

> "But when they believed Philip as he preached the things concerning the kingdom of God and the name of Jesus Christ, both men and women were baptized" (Acts 8:12).

Paul preached the kingdom of God and also about entering it

> "And he went into the synagogue and spoke boldly for three months, reasoning and persuading concerning the things of the kingdom of God" (Acts 19:8).

> "'And indeed, now I know that you all, among whom I have gone preaching the kingdom of God, will see my face no more'" (Acts 20:25).

> "So when they had appointed him a day, many came to him at *his* lodging, to whom he explained and solemnly testified of the kingdom of God, persuading them concerning Jesus from both the Law of Moses and the Prophets, from morning till evening" (Acts 28:23).

> "Then Paul dwelt two whole years in his own rented house, and received all who came to him, preaching the kingdom of God and teaching the things which concern the Lord Jesus Christ with all confidence, no one forbidding him" (Acts 28:30-31).

> "Strengthening the souls of the disciples, exhorting *them* to continue in the faith, and *saying,* "We must through many tribulations enter the kingdom of God" (Acts 14:22).

When there are that many references to the apostles preaching the kingdom of God, it is difficult to understand why so-called theologians have a problem approving the message of the kingdom today. It has always been the religious system and the religious spirit that opposes the message of the kingdom of God. When you see someone who does not like the message of the kingdom, it is evidence that a religious spirit is operating in that person. When Jesus was here on earth the Gentiles and the sinners did not oppose Him or what He preached. It was the religious leaders who opposed Him and did not like what He preached. Some things have not changed.

Have you ever wondered how twelve men in the first century reached the entire known world in their lifetime with the gospel of the kingdom? More than one billion believers have been trying to do this for decades and still half of the world remains unreached!

For three-and-a-half years, the main focus of Jesus' training and teaching to His disciples was the kingdom of God. Even after the resurrection, He talked with them about the kingdom for forty days. Jesus' priority is His kingdom and to see the will of His Father accomplished.

Although the church would be the greatest enterprise God ever began, Jesus, who is the Head of the church, taught about it only twice in His entire recorded preaching and teaching. On the other hand, He mentioned His kingdom more than a hundred times in the four Gospels.

Jesus wanted His disciples to become familiar with how His kingdom operated. He wanted to create a kingdom mindset in them before they ever got to do anything with His church. He knew that without it the church wouldn't be effective. Only when we understand the kingdom can we clearly understand the purpose of the church. The church is here to administer God's kingdom, but if its leaders don't know what the kingdom is and of what it is made, how can they administer it?

To understand the doctrine of the church, we need to understand the doctrine of the kingdom of God first. If we do not understand the kingdom we won't understand the church. That is why Jesus taught about the kingdom more than He taught about the church. He needed to establish the kingdom before He established the church because the church is here to administer the kingdom. If there is no kingdom then there is no need of a church.

The Church: A Familiar Term

Some people think the concept of the church did not begin until His resurrection. That is not true. The church has been on the earth ever since kingdoms, or the kingdom of God, began to operate here. Every kingdom had a *church or ekklesia* (the Greek word for chur*ch*) that administered its policies and rules. Without a church a kingdom cannot operate, and without a kingdom a church will not survive.

The reason the disciples did not question Jesus about the church when He mentioned it was because they were familiar with the concept of kingdoms having an *ekklesia* from a historic perspective (Israel was a kingdom) and from the political climate in which they were living. They knew Jesus was a king and that every king needed an *ekklesia*. It was a political term used in the Greek world and was never used to address a group of people who worshiped, preached, or sang. It was used to represent a group of citizens who were called out from among the people by a king or a government to administer the political, judicial, economic, and social affairs of the kingdom for the people.

Every king and kingdom had an *ekklesia* that governed its affairs. Jesus added a spiritual dimension to His kingdom and *ekklesia* when He said, "I will build my church" (Matthew 16:18), because His kingdom is a spiritual kingdom. Jesus is King, so He needs an *ekklesia* to govern the affairs of His kingdom. That is why He started the church.

Each time Jesus mentioned the church He referred to a governing body, not a place of worship. He referred to a group of people who were assigned to exercise authority to solve problems both in *the spiritual* and in *the natural* world. In the political world of those days, the *ekklesia* was a group of people who were called out—or selected—from the general public to govern the affairs of a kingdom or a nation.

The disciples knew that every king had an *ekklesia* in his kingdom that governed his affairs. That's why they kept asking Jesus when He was going to set up His kingdom on the earth. They wanted to sit and rule with Him.[23] When we read the gospel of Matthew, we notice that it was after Jesus said He will build His *ekklesia* that the mother of James and John came with the request for her sons to sit on His right and on His left in His kingdom.[24] They wanted to be part of His *ekklesia*, the governing body of His kingdom, but they only understood the natural aspect of the term. That's what they were familiar with at that time. The spiritual revelation of His kingdom or *ekklesia* came to them later.

Preparing for the Kingdom

Jesus wanted His disciples to have a kingdom perspective, a kingdom worldview. He wanted them to see the world through that kingdom paradigm before they got to do anything with the church. To prepare them, day and night He taught, preached, and trained them for three and a half years about how the kingdom worked. By the time the church started they had a kingdom mindset. That is why they were able to reach the whole known world with the gospel of the kingdom. Wherever they went and whatever they did, they did it according to a kingdom mindset, thus the church came out of the kingdom.

When we receive the kingdom as a whole and administer it effectively in our communities and nations, then the change we are looking for will happen. If we train our children to do the same, the ground we gain will be retained for generations to come. That is God's heart and that is the mandate of the kingdom of God.

The kingdom of God is an invisible kingdom. We cannot see with our natural eyes how it operates on the earth. He put His kingdom inside of us and it manifests to the world through the work we do. It is God's desire

---

23 See Matthew 20:21 and Acts 1:6.

24 See Matthew 20:20-21.

that His will is done *on this earth as it is in heaven*. This can only be done through human beings because the earth was given to us. The new era of the kingdom of God began to operate with the coming of the Holy Spirit on the day of Pentecost. The *ekklesia* of Jesus' kingdom began to operate from that day. We do not see anyone preaching that the kingdom is at hand after the day of Pentecost.

When we think of the church, we should think about it with a kingdom mindset. Before the *ekklesia* can operate, there has to be a kingdom. If there is no kingdom then there is no need of an *ekklesia* to govern it. That is why He came to give us the kingdom first, and preached and taught about it more than anything else. The problem today is there are many so-called *ekklesias* out there operating without proper knowledge of the kingdom. That is why we are not effective.

The Components of the Kingdom

If the church is here to administer God's kingdom, how do we do it in a practical sense? If God is making a "kingdom move" on the earth today, how does each believer take part in it?

The question is, what is the gospel of the kingdom? In order to understand the gospel of the kingdom we need to know what a kingdom is and what it is made of. A kingdom is a nation ruled by a king, a king's domain. This is a territory in which a king rules and where his will and purpose is accomplished. God wants to establish His will on the earth. His will is to be done *on earth as it is in heaven*.

If we are supposed to seek the kingdom first and the church is here to administer the kingdom of God, then we need to know what comprises a kingdom. A kingdom is made of twelve different components: 1) King, 2) Government/*Ekklesia*, 3) Territory, 4) Family, 5) Culture, 6) Decrees and Laws, 7) Army, 8) Education/Teachings, 9) Economy/Treasury, 10) Business/Industry, 11) Media, and 12) Agriculture.

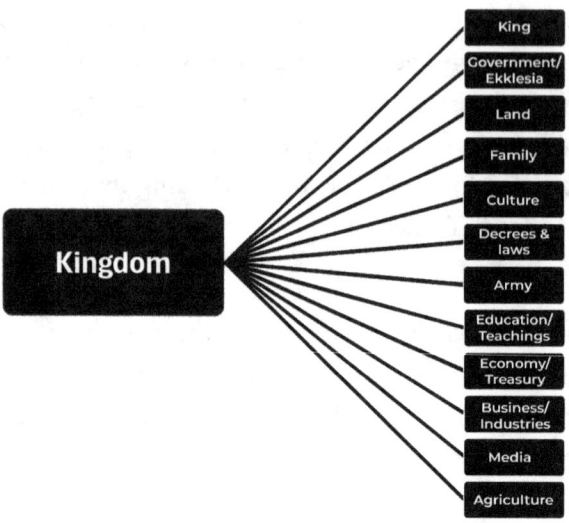

In the Bible, twelve is the number of divine government. When you hear the term *kingdom of God* I would like you to imagine all twelve ingredients, not just one or two of them, all working together to make a kingdom. There is a reason why there are twelve tribes of Israel and why Jesus selected twelve disciples. The hundred and twenty in the Upper Room is also twelve multiplied by ten. The three thousand souls that were saved on the Day of Pentecost is two hundred and fifty times twelve, and the twenty-four elders around the throne in heaven is twelve times two. Everything God does has a kingdom flavor.

If we study the book of Acts in detail, all twelve components of a kingdom were set in place as the church began to operate. They functioned as a kingdom under King Jesus.

1: The King

The first and most important component of a kingdom is the king. Jesus promised us that where two or three are gathered in His name, He will be there in their midst.[25] He also promised His disciples that though He

---

25 See Matthew 18:20.

would be taken away from them for a little while, He would come back to them.[26] In the book of Acts, God is referred to as the Holy Spirit and sometimes as Jesus because the Father, Son, and the Holy Spirit are all one. The concept of the trinity is there even though the word is not used.

2: The Government

The second component is the government. The church is the governing body of the kingdom of God. The book of Acts is all about this and how the apostles practiced it in the first century. The early church operated as a kingdom. We will go into this more in a later section.

3: Territory

The third component of a kingdom is territory. Before Jesus ascended to heaven He commissioned the disciples and told them the span of the territory that He wanted them to take His message. In Acts 1:8, He told them that after the Holy Spirit came upon them they would be His witnesses in Jerusalem, Judea, Samaria, and to the ends of the earth. When the Holy Spirit came, there were people from every nation under heaven in Jerusalem to witness it.[27]

They went from town to town, city to city, and nation to nation, preaching the gospel of the kingdom and overthrowing the kingdom (and the powers) of darkness, establishing the will of their King.

4: Family

The fourth component of a kingdom is family, or people. There were a hundred and twenty people, both men and women, including husbands and wives, in the upper room when the Holy Spirit came. On the Day

---

26 See John 16:16-17.

27 See Acts 2:5.

of Pentecost three thousand souls were saved and the *ekklesia* officially began to function.

5: Culture

The fifth component of a kingdom is culture. Those who became part of the *ekklesia* had a different culture than the other citizens of the country. Righteousness, love, peace, and joy in the Holy Spirit was their culture. They shared everything in common. They had a different culture than the people outside of the church.

6: Decrees and Laws

The sixth component of a kingdom is the decrees and laws of the king. When the Holy Spirit came, it was Peter who began to proclaim, under the power of the Holy Spirit, the words Jesus put in his heart to speak. He was not waiting there with a prepared message with notes and references. He had no idea what he was going to say, nor did he know he would be preaching that day. Those were the decrees and laws the King announced to the public.

When the church began, they functioned under the doctrine of the apostles, the decrees and laws of the kingdom. Whatever the King wanted to communicate, He communicated through the apostles, His ambassadors. When they sent a message to another group of believers, the message was called a decree. Only kings and kingdoms issue decrees.

> "And as they went through the cities, they delivered to them the decrees to keep, which were determined by the apostles and elders at Jerusalem" (Acts 16:4).

7: The Army

The seventh component of a kingdom is the army. Every believer was a soldier and the apostles were like generals in the army. This was a different kind of army, and they did not fight with swords and spears, but they had authority over all other kingdoms and kings in the natural and in the spirit. We see that many times when the apostles were arrested and put in prison by the rulers of a natural kingdom, the *ekklesia* prayed and cancelled the rule and authority of those kingdoms and governments.[28]

8: Education and Teaching

The eighth component of a kingdom is education. I don't have to explain this much because Jesus commanded them to go into all the world and teach all nations everything He taught them.[29] In Acts, we see the teachings of the apostles. The epistles are full of teaching and training from Paul, Peter, John and others for the *ekklesia*.

9: The Economy or Treasury

The ninth component of a kingdom is the economy/treasury. Seeing how this was handled in the early church is the most interesting part to me because we spend so much time making money for our survival. There was not a single believer in the early church who had an unmet need. How did that happen? What kind of financial system did they use? They established a kingdom economy to meet the needs of every single member in the church.

What they did was set up a *kingdom banking* system to meet the needs of the church. I thought it was a *welfare system* to help the poor, but later, when the Holy Spirit opened my eyes to the kingdom, I understood that it was a banking system. In a kingdom, the wealth of the kingdom is a literal commonwealth, meaning that all the wealth is available to everyone.

---

28 See Acts 5:17-20; 12:3-11; and 16:20-26.

29 Matthew 28:20.

This is not the same meaning[30] used today in nations that call themselves commonwealths. They do not function as the church did.

I used to think that when the church began in Acts 2, everybody sold everything they had and brought the money to the apostles and they all waited around in the temple for Jesus to come back. That is not what happened. Most of them only sold a portion of their possessions, house, or land, and brought it to the apostles. They distributed it as need arose and there was no one in the early church who had an unmet need. That is kingdom living.

> "Now the multitude of those who believed were of one heart and one soul; neither did anyone say that any of the things he possessed was his own, but they had all things in common. And with great power the apostles gave witness to the resurrection of the Lord Jesus. And great grace was upon them all. Nor was there anyone among them who lacked; for all who were possessors of lands or houses sold them, and brought the proceeds of the things that were sold, and laid *them* at the apostles' feet; and they distributed to each as anyone had need" (Acts 4:32-35).

If they had sold everything they had, they could not have met from house to house every day. The following verse says they sold possessions and goods, referring to real estate and products, and they met from house to house daily.

> "Now all who believed were together, and had all things in common, and sold their possessions and goods, and divided them among all, as anyone had need. So continuing daily with one accord in the temple, and breaking

---

30 "Commonwealth - Dictionary Definition," Vocabulary.com, accessed February 15, 2017, https://www.vocabulary.com/dictionary/commonwealth.

Chapter 4 | The Book of Acts from a Kingdom Perspective

bread from house to house, they ate their food with gladness and simplicity of heart" (Acts 2:44-46).

"And daily in the temple, and in every house, they did not cease teaching and preaching Jesus *as* the Christ" (Acts 5:42).

I believe when every *ekklesia* reaches three thousand people (that's when it happened in the early church), they should start their own banking system. We should not depend on the economy of this world, but show the world how a kingdom economy operates.

On the day of Pentecost, three thousand souls were saved, and the New Testament church was born. Imagine an *ekklesia* with three thousand members at the present day. If they are all working to support their families, each of them would have income and a bank account. If that church is in the United States where an average person makes twenty thousand dollars a year (I know most people make more than that and I am just taking the least amount), and if you multiply three thousand by twenty thousand the total comes to sixty million dollars a year. Wow! It could be closer to a hundred million or even more because most people make significantly more than twenty thousand a year. That's the minimum amount of money that would come and go through that body in a year. That is a lot of money! And, that's just one local church.

What if that church had a banking system to manage that much money instead of depending on a bank that is run by unbelievers that are using our money to support the kingdom of darkness and its agenda? If you calculate all the money you make and the money you spend, you will see that most of your money goes back into the pockets of the ungodly. The wicked become wealthier and wealthier while the righteous come to church and cry out every day for a financial breakthrough. Lord, have mercy! What if we had a system to keep our money within the kingdom of God? We need to use the wisdom and knowledge of our God to create and manage wealth. We need to study kingdom economy. It is the church that makes the ungodly wealthy but we do not recognize it. We have been blinded by the devil.

It will take wisdom and a lot of planning and trained individuals to do this. That's how it happened in the early church. Imagine that three thousand people sold part of their possessions, goods, houses, or land, and brought the money and put it at the feet of the apostles. How much money was it? Who managed all that money? What was the system they used to do it? It's called kingdom economy. In the early church, they did not borrow money from the world to buy a house or to send their children to school. That is totally unacceptable in the kingdom of God.

It is important to notice that they sold possessions and goods. To whom did they sell these? I am sure it was to the people in the church and outside the church. We need to encourage believers to come up with products that they can sell to generate income. That's the way we tap into the wealth of the wicked and create money for kingdom purpose.

If a particular kingdom citizen goes to a different kingdom to borrow money for their livelihood, to build a house, or for anything, who does that affect most? The king in that kingdom. It affects his reputation because it demonstrates the king's inability to meet the needs of his people. That is what we have been doing for a long time, but no more. In Acts and the epistles, I do not see any believer who is a kingdom citizen going out and borrowing money from unbelievers for anything.

The book of Acts should be our blueprint for running a church, because it operated like a kingdom. When one church had a financial struggle, or was affected by famine, another church that was doing well sent help and support.[31] This way their wealth always stayed in the church or in the kingdom. We have much to learn about kingdom economy. When

---

31 See Acts 11:28-29; 1 Corinthians 16:1-4; and 2 Corinthians 9:1-5.

the whole church is united, as Jesus wants it to be, we will be the largest economic force on the planet. If the church in each nation is united, they will be the largest economic force in that nation. Then we could lend money to unbelievers and invest in different projects. That money would be used to support the church and its ministries, rather than the tithes coming from believers. There would be no needs that were not met in our churches just as it was in the early church. That is what the Bible tells us. We should be lending and not borrowing because we represent and live in the most prosperous kingdom.

The devil knows more about God, His kingdom, and how it operates than most Christians, including preachers, because he was with Him and knew Him personally. I am currently working on a book about kingdom economy, which should be released sometime in 2018. The subtitle of that book is *Why All Tithe-Giving Believers Do Not Receive a Financial Breakthrough*. Please make sure you get it and read it. I am asking you to spread the news about this kingdom message to your friends and family. People are tired of religion and rituals. They are looking for something real, something that works.

What the Holy Spirit is sharing with you through this book are seeds of the kingdom. It's up to you to nurture, research, study, and pray to receive more revelation on each of these subjects. It's time for us to change the way we do church. Actually, it's kind of late to change. We need to tear down the religious strongholds and root the enemy out of our lives and begin again.

10: Media

The tenth component of the kingdom is the media. During the first century there was no electronic media as we use today. The only media available were preaching and writing. We see in the book of Acts they were busy using both. We should utilize and maximize every form of media that is available to spread the gospel of the kingdom.

11: Business and Industry

The eleventh component of the kingdom is business/industry. As the church grew, believers began to do business and people who were in business were added to the church. We read about prominent men and women that were won to Christ by the apostles. Many of them excelled in business and politics, and prospered. Paul was a tent-maker. He supported his ministry team and personal life through that business.

Dorcas and Lydia were businesswomen.[32] They had products they sold. I am sure there were others who were doing business. One of Paul's primary admonitions was to do good works. The phrase *good works* appears twenty-eight times in the New Testament. The Greek word for "work" is *ergon*, which means "to work, business, employment, that with which anyone is occupied. Any product whatever, anything accomplished by hand, art, industry, or mind."[33]

The Bible refers to our natural gift, trade, or occupation as our good works.

"For we are His workmanship, created in Christ Jesus for *good works*, which God prepared beforehand that we should walk in them" (Ephesians 2:10).

In the church, we have limited good works to things like helping orphans, feeding the poor, or visiting nursing homes and prisons, instead of its real and fuller meaning. *Anything* you do that is productive and fruitful is a good work. Any work that God gave you to do is a good work. That means that a mother caring for her children is doing a good work and pleasing to God. Similarly, the person who works and develops his talents in any field is pleasing God. Jesus and Paul tell believers again and again to engage themselves in good works.

---

32 See Acts 9:39 and 16:14.

33 James Strong, "Strong's Greek: 2041, ἔργον (ergon) – work," Strong's Greek: 2041, ἔργον (ergon) – work, accessed February 15, 2017, http://biblehub.com/greek/2041.htm.

One of the ways Jesus said people will glorify our heavenly Father is by seeing our good works. We, the children of God, are supposed to be the most productive people on earth.

> "Let your light so shine before men, that they may see your good works and glorify your Father in heaven" (Matthew 5:16).

The light Jesus refers to in the above verse is our good works. He also said that we are the light of the world.[34] That means if anything good is going to happen it has to come through us. The Lord told me a few years ago that He wanted to release every new invention through one of His children, through His church, but that His children were all busy singing and waiting for a revival or the rapture. Therefore, He had to choose an unbeliever to release the idea, and they are making billions of dollars with it.

12: Agriculture

The twelfth component of a kingdom is agriculture. We cannot live without food. The early church grew to thousands and thousands of people in the first few months. They fed all those people. Jesus their King taught them how to feed a multitude and how to manage big crowds.

In the Gospels when the people were hungry, Jesus told His disciples to feed them.[35] Their idea was to collect some money and go to the next town and buy food to feed the five thousand men plus women and children. But that was not Jesus' plan. He has provision in His kingdom to feed the entire world each day. He taught them a very important lesson that day, one we all need to practice: Don't depend on the world for our food supply. Depend on His kingdom and produce our own food. I do not believe Jesus would do a miracle every day to feed us, but He gives us ideas of how to produce our food and we can put them to work.

---

34 See Matthew 5:14.

35 See Luke 9:19.

We also read in Acts that believers used to meet in the temple and break bread from house to house daily. There arose a complaint in Acts 6 about the fairness of the daily food distribution, so the apostles selected leaders to take care of the problem.

Influencing Earth with Heaven

When you read the book of Acts with a kingdom mindset, you can see that all the aspects of the kingdom were active in the early church. They functioned as a kingdom would function and not as a religious or charitable organization. They put into practice what Jesus had taught them. The Holy Spirit had empowered them to administer God's kingdom here.

That's why they were able to reach the entire known world in their lifetime. Today, we are trying to reach the world with a church or religious mindset and we are not that effective.

The gospel of the kingdom affects every aspect of society. It is not focused on just taking people to heaven. We do not see Jesus or His disciples preaching with the goal of taking people to heaven anywhere in the Gospels or in Acts. None of their messages ended by asking people, "How many of you want to receive Jesus and go to heaven? Please raise your hands." Nobody preached like that in the Bible.

There are people who are saved and attend churches worldwide, but many are hungry and broke and their families and countries are in shambles. What is the solution? The gospel of the kingdom. They only heard the gospel of salvation. Some evangelist went there and preached and they accepted Jesus so they could go to heaven and they are waiting for Him to come and fetch them away.

The focus of the gospel of the kingdom is supposed to be to influence earth with heaven. That is our primary goal. That is the primary focus of the prayer Jesus taught us to pray, which most of us do not pray anymore. We are to influence the culture of earth with the culture of heaven.

Chapter 4 | The Book of Acts from a Kingdom Perspective

Every nation has the twelve components I mentioned above, but they are not real; only the kingdom of God has the real stuff. When we administer the kingdom of God to the nations of the world, we will see them come to Christ one by one. As a result, Jesus will return. The question is, "How do we administer His kingdom?" In the following pages I will explain that according to the grace God has given me. This book is only a seed. I pray that as you read, the Holy Spirit will reveal more details to you.

Jesus said, "When this gospel of the kingdom shall be preached as a witness to all nations then the end will come." Jesus and the disciples preached the gospel of the kingdom. Which gospel are we preaching these days? Every denomination seems to have its own version of the gospel. There is the Baptist gospel, Pentecostal gospel, Catholic gospel, and many others. When we preach the gospel of the kingdom then the end will come.

Chapter 5

Administering the Kingdom of God, Part 1

"That Your way may be known on earth, Your salvation among all nations" (Psalm 67:2).

To restore a nation back to God we need to understand the system by which a nation operates. When you influence that system with the kingdom of God, you will reach that nation. Let's examine how to administer the kingdom of God based on the twelve components we just studied.

If you study the parables Jesus shared, you will notice He used one of these natural components by which a kingdom is made to reveal the spiritual principles that govern our life in His kingdom. Jesus is exceedingly wise. Whatever He does or says has to have a kingdom purpose. Two of the most famous parables are about a sower sowing seed and the parable of the Perfect Father, which we call the parable of the prodigal son. One of those parables is connected to kingdom agriculture and the other to kingdom family.

Below is a list of a few of the parables that are connected to each of the twelve components of the kingdom. The rest you find out on your own during your personal study. Do a little research on and discover the depth of His Word.

The King

- Parable of the king and his servants in Matthew 18:23-35.
- Parable of the king and the marriage feast in Matthew 22:1-14.

Territory/Land

- Parable of the landowner and hired servants in Matthew 20:1-16.
- Parable of the landowner and the vineyard in Matthew 21:33-46.

Culture

- Parable of the Good Samaritan in Luke 10:25-37.
- Parable of the friends at midnight in Luke 11:1-10.
- Parable of the birds and lilies in Matthew 6:25-34.

Government

- Parable of the rock and keys in Matthew 16:15-19.
- Parable of the unrighteous judge in Luke 18:1-8.

Decrees and Laws

Every parable in the Gospels contains decrees and laws of the kingdom of God. Jesus used parables to reveal the mysteries of His kingdom.

Family

- Parable of the perfect father in Luke 15:11-32.

- Parable of the two sons and the vineyard in Matthew 21:28-32.
- Parable of the marriage feast and wedding garment in Matthew 22:1-14.

Economy

- Parable of the treasure and the field in Matthew 13:44.
- Parable of the talents and rewards in Matthew 25:14-30.
- Parable of the faithful steward in Luke 16:1-13.

Education

- Parable of the scribe and the householder in Matthew 13:51-52.
- All of Jesus' teachings are part of some form of kingdom education.

Army

- Parable of the king going to war in Luke 14:31-32.

Business and Industries

- Parable of the merchant and the pearl in Matthew 13:45-46.
- Parable of the faithful and wise servant in Matthew 24:45-51.
- Parable of the ten virgins in Matthew 25:1-13.
- Parable of the tower builder in Luke 14:25-30.
- Parable of the unrighteous steward in Luke 16:1-13.
- Parable of the nobleman and his ten servants in Luke 19:11-17.

Media

There is no need of any specific reference to media because whatever Jesus preached and taught was through the medium of speech and what others wrote.

Agriculture

There are more parables connected to agriculture and economy than any of the other areas. I believe this is because those two areas were connected to the lives of the people of that day more closely than others. They are also part of the foundation of kingdom economy.

- Parable of the Sower and the seed in Matthew 13:3-23.
- Parable of the mustard tree and the birds in Matthew 13:31-32.
- Parable of the leaven and meal in Matthew 13:33-35.
- Parable of the good and bad fish in Matthew 13:47-50.
- Parable of the sheep and goats in Matthew 25:31-46.

Now let's see how to administer the kingdom of God so that we can see nations being restored to God. As you read, I pray that this revelation will be deposited into your spirit and take root in your life so that you will be able to discover which area you are called to influence and see your part in restoring your nation.

The King of All Kings

The most important component of a kingdom is the king. In this case, Jesus is our King. He is not just a king but He is called the King of Kings. He is the only person who is a King from birth.

Every nation has a government, and most nations are facing the problem of a failed government. People are tired of their government, and they are complaining about their leaders and their corruption. What is the solution? The solution is to raise up a new generation of people who will witness Jesus as a king. What do kings do? They govern.

"The Lord *is King* forever and ever" (Psalm 10:16a).

"For the *king*dom *is* the Lord's, and He rules over the nations" (Psalm 22:28).

He is also called the King of glory.[36]

> "Where is He who has been born **King** of the Jews? For we have seen His star in the East and have come to worship Him" (Matthew 2:2).

> "Now to the **King** eternal, immortal, invisible, to God who alone is wise, *be* honor and glory forever and ever. Amen" (1 Timothy 1:17).

There were many in the Old Testament who witnessed God as King on the earth. Why don't we see this in our day? Did God cease from being a king?

> "For unto us a Child is born, unto us a Son is given; and the government will be upon His shoulder. And His name will be called Wonderful, Counselor, Mighty God, Everlasting Father, Prince of Peace. Of the increase of *His* government and peace *there will be* no end, upon the throne of David and over His kingdom, to order it and establish it with judgment and justice from that time forward, even forever. The zeal of the Lord of hosts will perform this" (Isaiah 9:6-7).

This is a prophetic declaration about our Lord Jesus Christ. It says that the government will be upon His shoulder. It does not say the economy, evangelism, or the business shall be on His shoulders, but government. A nation rises or falls based on its government.

How does government rest upon His shoulders? He is the Head of the church and we are His body on the earth. The shoulder is part of the body, which means the government of this earth is supposed to be on the shoulders of the church. Throughout the Bible it was always a priest or

---

36 See Psalm 24:8.

a prophet who appointed kings, the political leaders, not the other way around. For some reason, we made this verse part of our eschatology, meaning something that is going to take place somewhere out there in the future. This is not true according to the verse.

That is what religion does. It steals from us what we should have now and gives us a false hope that someday things are going to be better. But faith says, "Now."

From the phrase, "From that time forward, even forever," we understand that the fulfillment of the prophetic timing began from the time a Son was given. It says that of the increase of His government and peace, there will be no end. That means it is eternal. We all know the Son spoken of here is Jesus. He came two thousand years ago and He is going to order His government with judgment and justice from that time forward, even forever. It literally began two thousand years ago, but we have not grasped what that really means.

Witnessing Jesus as the King

The prophecy in Isaiah began to be fulfilled with the announcement of the angel to Mary, his mother, in Luke 1.

> "He will be great, and will be called the Son of the Highest; and the Lord God will give Him the throne of His father David. And He will reign over the house of Jacob forever, and of His kingdom there will be no end" (Luke 1:32-33).

When the wise men from the East came to see Jesus, they came looking for the King who was born in Bethlehem. How did they receive the revelation that Jesus was a king? Because of His star they saw in the East. When He died, He died as a king too. The inscription on the cross was "King of the Jews." When the governor asked Jesus if He was the King of the Jews, He did not deny it. He said, "It is as you say."[37]

---

37 See Matthew 27:11.

One of the complaints against the church in the book of Acts was that they were preaching another king other than Caesar, and issuing different decrees.

> "But when they did not find them, they dragged Jason and some brethren to the rulers of the city, crying out, 'These who have turned the world upside down have come here too. Jason has harbored them, and these are all acting contrary to the decrees of Caesar, saying there is another king—Jesus.' And they troubled the crowd and the rulers of the city when they heard these things" (Acts 17:6-8)

How do we witness to others about Jesus as the King? Believers need to be involved in the political arena of their nations. We have been avoiding politics for too long, and because of that, the unrighteous have taken over governments all over the world. There is no such thing as a righteous justice system in the world anymore. People with money make their own rules. Any wicked person with money can do almost anything anywhere in the world.

Isaiah said the government shall be upon the shoulder of Jesus,[38] not on the shoulder of the devil. Church leaders should encourage believers to get involved in politics, both locally and in the central government of their nations. Otherwise, how do we witness to others that Jesus is King?

One of the main reasons this world is in chaos is because there are not very many people witnessing Jesus as the King. "When the righteous are in authority, the people rejoice; but when a wicked *man* rules, the people groan" (Proverbs 29:2).

Go Back to the Roots

Any time I meet someone from any country, they are always complaining about how bad the government in their nation is doing. They speak

---

38 See Isaiah 9:6.

negatively about their leaders. This will not change anything for the better. The only way to change anything is if we have witnesses for Jesus in those governments. We need believers in positions of influence striving for kingdom causes. We must find out why we do not have any influence in government and come up with a solution.

One of the popular messages of the last few years has been to tell Americans to go back to its roots; that message is dying out as I write this book. America cannot go back to its roots by just preaching about it. We need a new strategy.

There were fifty-six men who signed the Declaration of Independence. Out of the fifty-six, *all* of them were known to be Christians and attended some form of church.[39] That meant their moral and ethical value systems were based on Biblical ethics. That is why this country was established the way it was. How many people do we have in our government now with those kind of ethics? If we are going to take this country back to its roots, we need believers in positions of government—at the local, state, and national levels—who will witness Jesus as the King. This is beginning to happen.

We are not here to take over governments, but like Joseph and Daniel did, we need to have people with influence in high places. Every single person God has ever used manifested Christ and His mission on earth through their lives. We have received the real deal, and today there are fewer witnesses for Jesus than ever in world governments.

Government Workers Are Ministers

God has anointed many people with His power to be a witness in government, but they have avoided it, thinking it is not God's will for them. The

---

[39] "Religious Affiliation of the Signers of the Declaration of Independence," Religious Affiliation of the Signers of the Declaration of Independence, accessed February 15, 2017, http://www.freerepublic.com/focus/news/2546951/posts.

enemy has deceived us to keep us out of this most important aspect of a nation, so that he can have free rein. Every government on earth belongs to Jesus, because there is no authority, natural or spiritual, except from Him. Why should we give the authority God gave us to the devil and then complain about what he is doing with it? Paul calls people in governmental authority "ministers." Did you know that? In Romans 13 he mentioned it twice. I was really surprised when I first read this.

"For he is God's minister to you for good" (Romans 13:4a).

"For because of this you also pay taxes, for they are God's ministers attending continually to this very thing" (Romans 13:6).

I am a minister of the gospel. I preach the gospel to groups of people. If you are in charge of finance in the government of your nation, then you are also a minister of God. You preach the gospel through your influence, your input, and your decisions. The same Holy Spirit is working through us, but in different manifestations.

Each believer is anointed to manifest at least one aspect of Jesus. When we all come together as a body, we have the fullness of God.[40] Church, this has to happen. It must happen if Jesus is going to return to the earth. He is not coming for a church that is fractured into a million pieces and crying like a baby to get out of the earth. He is coming for a victorious church.

Every person God used in the Old Testament was a type or shadow of Christ. That means they were representing or foreshadowing Christ who was to come. Abraham was a prophet, Joseph was a prime minister, and David was a king. Esther was a queen, Moses was a deliverer, and the list goes on. They were all witnesses of the Messiah. Jesus is all of these and more. Jesus said that every Scripture testifies of Him.

---

40 See Ephesians 4:13.

> "You search the Scriptures, for in them you think you have eternal life; and these are they which *testify* of Me" (John 5:39).

His kingdom and dominion is for now and forever. Many are waiting for the millennial reign to reign with Jesus. You are destined to reign now on this earth. Jesus wants to reign on the earth through His church. We need to start schools in every nation that train people to reign, and to get involved with local and federal government. We have prophetic schools that train people to prophesy. We have healing schools that train people to heal sicknesses. Why don't we have governing and business schools that train people how to get involved in the government and start businesses? We must do this if we are going to bring any change in our nations.

When God created the earth, to whom did he give the earth and its reign? To Adam, right? What would we be doing on this earth if Adam did not fall? After Adam, who was going to rule the earth? His sons, and after his sons, then who? Their sons. Where in the Bible does it say God gave the governing authority to the devil or the unrighteous? Nowhere.

The enemy knows this, and for too long he has deceived the church to keep them away from government. Who said kings can only do business but they cannot be involved in government? What an incredible deception!

This idea is based on Old Testament concepts and theology. There was a clear separation between the offices of king, priest, and prophet in the Old Testament. In the New Testament, a child of God is a king, priest, and a prophet all at the same time! In our relationship with God we are His children, but in our position on earth we are kings first. What does a king do? Possess the land and rule or govern.

Releasing Kings to Their Original Intent

The reason most nations are going from bad to worse is because the people who are anointed by God to be kings are not occupying their place and

Chapter 5 | Administering the Kingdom of God, Part 1

space. There is a false teaching in the body of Christ that says kings are those who do business in the market place. They reduced the capacity and the power of kings to just making money. This happened because of the influence of the spirit of mammon and love for money.

Prosperity teaching brought the love of money to the mainstream. Common sense tells us that kings are those who rule and govern a territory. They are not running around in the marketplace, witnessing and praying for the sick. Their witness needs to be in the arena of government.

I am here to declare and release kings to God's original intent. When the kings take their place in every culture and nation, we will see the long awaited transformation.

There is a misconception among the body of Christ that believers are allowed to do business, watch movies, go to parties and do whatever they want to do, but they should not enter into politics. I wonder who came up with such an idea.

There were more people in the Bible that God used in the arena of government and to influence governments than any other purpose. Today we have the least amount of believers involved in governments or influencing governments. There are more believers sitting in our pews that are called to be in government and to influence governments, but they have been wrongly taught or haven't been taught at all about their calling and their purpose. They are frustrated and angry about what is going on in their nation and feel stuck. These people need to be released into their purpose and calling. Churches need to remove the limitations they have put on these leaders and let them be the agents of change. God created them to be influencers outside the church.

To do this, we need to train kings to be in positions of government and execute God's purpose in those regions. To know more about kings and their responsibilities, please read the book, *Releasing Kings and Queens to Their Original Intent*. You can order it at www.TheKingdomNetwork.org

Kingdom Government

I wrote a lot about kingdom government in *The Power and Authority of the Church*. Please refer to the chapter called *Ekklesia* to know how the government and governing body of the kingdom work. I will add here some things that I did not mention in that book. A king is the most important person in a kingdom. Jesus Christ is our King. In every kingdom, there are elders serving under the king. They are appointed to oversee different aspects or departments in the kingdom. Have you ever wondered why there are twenty-four elders in heaven? They are the governing body of the kingdom in heaven.[41]

In the Old Testament, the nation of Israel and every other kingdom had elders who worked under the king and at each of the city gates. They made decisions and ran the day-to-day affairs of the people, representing the king.[42]

> "Then Peter, filled with the Holy Spirit, said to them, 'Rulers of the people and elders of Israel'" (Acts 4:8)

The church is supposed to be functioning as a kingdom, not a democracy. That is the way it functioned in the book of Acts. The church is the governing body of the kingdom of God on earth. If you study the New Testament, you will notice that the churches Paul established were led by groups of elders.

Each time Paul established a church he appointed elders who did the work of a pastor. They were called elders and not pastors. We call them pastors today. Those churches worked under the apostolic leadership of Paul and his team. *There was always a plurality of leadership in a local church.*

> "So when they had appointed elders in every church, and prayed with fasting, they commended them to the Lord in whom they had believed" (Acts 14:23).

---

41 See Revelation 4:4.

42 See Genesis 50:7 and Exodus 3:16 and 24:1.

> "And when they had come to Jerusalem, they were received by the church and the apostles and the elders; and they reported all things that God had done with them" (Acts 15:4).

> "From Miletus he sent to Ephesus and called for the elders of the church"(Acts 20:17).

It was the elders who governed and taught the Word.

> "Let the elders who rule well be counted worthy of double honor, especially those who labor in the word and doctrine" (1 Timothy 5:17).

> "For this reason I left you in Crete, that you should set in order the things that are lacking, and appoint elders in every city as I commanded you" (Titus 1:15).

It was the elders who prayed for the sick.

> "Is anyone among you sick? Let him call for the elders of the church, and let them pray over him, anointing him with oil in the name of the Lord" (James 5:14).

The apostles also called themselves elders in the later part of their ministry.

> "The elders who are among you I exhort, I who am a fellow elder and a witness of the sufferings of Christ, and also a partaker of the glory that will be revealed" (1 Peter 5:1).

> "Likewise you younger people, submit yourselves to *your* elders. Yes, all of *you* be submissive to one another, and be clothed with humility, for 'God resists the proud, But gives grace to the humble'" (1 Peter 5:5).

We need to keep in mind (and remind ourselves constantly) that the church belongs to Jesus Christ. He said, "I will build My church." He also promised that when we gather He will be there in our midst. If that is true, every time we gather we need to acknowledge Him as our King and Lord who is present among us and yield to Him, allowing Him to do whatever He chooses. The church is never supposed to be centered around a human personality; it must be centered around the One to Whom it belongs.

When the Corinthian church began to focus on a human personality, Paul rebuked them harshly.

> "For it has been declared to me concerning you, my brethren, by those of Chloe's *household,* that there are contentions among you. Now I say this, that each of you says, 'I am of Paul,' or 'I am of Apollos,' or 'I am of Cephas,' or 'I am of Christ.' Is Christ divided? Was Paul crucified for you? Or were you baptized in the name of Paul?" (1 Corinthians 1:11-13).

The church is not about apostles, prophets, evangelist, pastors, and teachers. It is about Jesus the King and His kingdom. It's time for us to get out of the way and bring the King back to His original place in the church.

We, the church, have missed it big time on two fronts. First, we became so heaven-focused that we missed the purpose God gave us to accomplish. Heaven does not need our help to make it a better place or to populate it. But the earth does. That is why we are here. Heaven is already a place of abundance and sufficiency. God did not create us to live or sing in heaven. When God created man He did not tell us, "Okay, now I want you to populate heaven for Me." No. He never said that.

Second, the church became all about man instead of the King. We've had all kinds of movements: the apostolic movement, the prophetic movement, the prosperity movement, and many others, but never a kingdom movement that was focused on Jesus and His kingdom. I believe the time has come. There was a Jesus movement but it was not focused on His kingdom here; it was all about taking people to heaven. At least it was about Jesus. Many of the older generation alive today came to the Lord through that movement.

The Bible clearly shows that elders under an apostolic covering ran the early church, and that there was more than one elder in every local church. When I labored under a religious spirit I saw only the miracles in the book of Acts, and they were my focus. I often wished the miracles done in the book of Acts could happen again so the world would be converted. I did not see that the reason the miracles took place was because they were signs of the kingdom of God, and that the early church was functioning as a kingdom is supposed to function.

Kingdom Territory

Once you understand the kingdom of God and your responsibility in His kingdom, you need to realize your connection with the land. If you have no revelation of the land and you do not feel any connection with the land you live in, then you do not have a real revelation of God or His kingdom.

To a king, the land and people determine his kingdom. The size of the land shows the size of his kingdom. If there is no land, there is no kingdom. If an enemy has taken over the land, then that king loses his kingdom. That is what happened to this earth. The enemy has taken the land from us.

Even today, when false religious groups enter a new region, the first thing they do is buy a prime piece of land to establish their center. They will not have a crusade or food distribution. They will establish a center and then they will start doing community works. I have heard that next to the U.S. government, the Church of Latter Day Saints (the Mormons or LDS) owns the largest amount of land in the United States west of the Mississippi River.[43]

---

43 Arizona Republic, "LDS CHURCH REAL-ESTATE HOLDINGS INCLUDE FARMS, RANCHES, BUILDINGS," DeseretNews.com, July 02, 1991, accessed February 15, 2017, http://www.deseretnews.com/article/170647/LDS-CHURCH-REAL-ESTATE-HOLDINGS-INCLUDE-FARMS-RANCHES-BUILDINGS.html.

We need to claim land like this too. God told Abraham to look and walk on the land and every piece of land he saw and walked upon, God said He would give to him (Genesis 13:14-17). We should believe and do the same. We have a God-given responsibility to care for the land and be good stewards of it.

The Land Needs to Be Healed

The Bible says the earth and its fullness belong to the Lord.[44] At the same time, it says that if God's people humble themselves, and pray and forsake their sins, then God will heal their land.[45] Why does the land need to be healed? We have been wrongly quoting this Scripture to support our revival syndrome for a long time.

The land was cursed because of the fall of man and lost its power to produce to its full capacity. It stopped yielding its strength. Instead, it began to produce thorns and thistles. Sin and the shedding of innocent blood pollute the land. If the land is to yield its strength again, we need to appropriate redemption to the land.

The devil will try his best to keep believers from owning any land. The biggest fight you will fight in your life will be to possess a piece of land. The first thing you need to do as a king and an heir of God on this earth is own a piece of land in your own name. It is the responsibility of each believer to possess a piece of land and invite King Jesus to come and rule over that property, and to release that property to Him for Him to use it to reign in that region. This is not a "me, mine, and I" philosophy. These are kingdom principles.

Once you own the land, it's up to the King to tell you what to do on it or with it. Sometimes He will tell you to give it away to someone who doesn't have any land. He may tell you to establish a business, ministry, school, nursing home, or to use it for agriculture. A believer that owns

---

44 See Psalm 24:1.

45 See 2 Chronicles 7:14.

land and does agriculture is also a king. Abraham, Isaac, and Jacob lived by agriculture. The Bible never called them farmers. They were living like kings and were called prophets and anointed of the Lord.

The Land Holds the Treasure of the Kingdom

When Jesus shared parables about the kingdom of God, He shared about buying and owning land because the treasure of the kingdom of heaven is hidden in the land. Few understand this. Everything you are and have is connected to land. Everything we eat and use comes from the land somehow or other. No land, no kingdom; no kingdom, no dominion.

> "Again, the kingdom of heaven is like treasure hidden in a field, which a man found and hid; and for joy over it he goes and sells all that he has and buys that field" (Matthew 13:44).

I was surprised by this parable. The man did not sell everything he had to buy the treasure, but bought the land because the treasure was hidden there. What was the treasure hidden in the field? It was the kingdom of heaven.

> "For the kingdom of heaven is like a landowner who went out early in the morning to hire laborers for his vineyard" (Matthew 20:1).

God wants you to be a landowner. God is the King of all the earth.[46] What is Earth? The physical planet. Why is God the King of all the earth? Because land is necessary in order to exercise dominion.

The Land Should Be Possessed

Every call and covenant of God is connected to land. It is our responsibility as the children of God to redeem and heal the land so that it will yield

---

46 See Psalm 47:2.

its strength once again, and produce food to eliminate hunger from the face of the earth. There is land in every nation lying vacant and desolate. As kingdom representatives, we are supposed to move into those regions to make those wildernesses into gardens of life.

> "I will open rivers in desolate heights, and fountains in the midst of the valleys; I will make the wilderness a pool of water, and the dry land springs of water" (Isaiah 41:18).

> "Behold, I will do a new thing, now it shall spring forth; shall you not know it? I will even make a road in the wilderness *and* rivers in the desert" (Isaiah 43:19).

> "For the Lord will comfort Zion, He will comfort all her waste places; He will make her wilderness like Eden, and her desert like the garden of the Lord; joy and gladness will be found in it, thanksgiving and the voice of melody" (Isaiah 51:3).

Less than ten percent of the landmass of earth is inhabited. As kings, we need to move into those vast areas of land and build new self-sustaining communities, towns, and cities. People complain about trouble and pollution in cities. Why can't we be like the patriarchs who established cities and nations? As God's children, we are supposed to possess the earth and make it like the garden of Eden for the benefit of humanity.

The Land Testifies of Wickedness

> "Because of the transgression of a land, many *are* its **princes**; but by a man of understanding *and* knowledge right will be prolonged" (Proverbs 28:2).

This verse is powerful. One of the problems in Third World countries is division in governments, families, and churches. This verse gives the clue to its reason. Because of the transgression of a land, many are its princes. Though we are all kings, we are not all called to be leaders of nations.

When there is so much transgression committed in an area, people cannot unite to achieve any goal. There will not be any unity. This is happening in the United States. There is much violence in our cities. People are protesting and destroying public property. These people do not know their purpose; they are just wandering in the streets.

There is no unity in the government or between communities because so much transgression has happened to the land and in the land. Now the land is refusing to submit. That is another reason for the increase in natural calamities in this nation as well.

> "Do not defile yourselves with any of these things; for by all these the nations are defiled, which I am casting out before you. For the land is defiled; therefore I visit the punishment of its iniquity upon it, and the land vomits out its inhabitants. You shall therefore keep My statutes and My judgments, and shall not commit *any* of these abominations, *either* any of your own nation or any stranger who dwells among you (for all these abominations the men of the land have done, who *were* before you, and thus the land is defiled), lest the land vomit you out also when you defile it, as it vomited out the nations that *were* before you" (Leviticus 18:24-28).

How can the land vomit out its inhabitants? Land is not a person or living creature, but the land has much more sensitivity and life in it than most people understand. The earth will itself testify of all of the wickedness that has been done on it. Moses said he called heaven and earth to be a witness against God's people.

> "I call heaven and earth to witness against you this day, that you will soon utterly perish from the land which you cross over the Jordan to possess; you will not prolong *your* days in it, but will be utterly destroyed" (Deuteronomy 4:26).

The land can mourn because of the sins of its inhabitants.[47] This is a theme throughout Scripture. When you buy a piece of land, make sure you redeem it from every curse that has been operating in it. Please "ask" its forgiveness for all the atrocities done on it. There are resources you can look up that will help you do that.

Every call and purpose of God is connected to a particular land. When God created Adam, He told him to subdue and have dominion over all the earth and everything He had created. Then God put the first man in a piece of land called the garden of Eden. The first man, Adam, lost that land and the dominion.

After the flood, God made a covenant with Noah and gave him and his children the entire earth. When God called Abraham He promised him land too. The Israelites were freed from slavery in Egypt and taken into a place called the Promised Land. It is time to take possession of the land that has been assigned to you too.

Kingdom Family

Family is the first institution God established on earth. It is the foundation of society, a nation, and a church. The devil hates family with all his being. He knows that if he can destroy the foundation, he can hurt everything else. I'd say he has been somewhat successful in doing so.

In this day and age, it is very difficult to find a real man or a real woman. What do I mean by that? According to modern thinking, just because we have an obvious sexual orientation, we are not necessarily a man or a woman. Just because someone is born male or female will not make them a man or a woman when they grow up.

---

47 See Isaiah 24:4-6; Jeremiah 4:28 and 12:4; and Hosea 4:3.

You get together with men these days and all they have to talk about is sports or entertainment. Women talk about shopping, their pets, and their children. Lord, have mercy! These are sons and daughters, kings and queens, God created to have dominion and expand His kingdom. No wonder the world is in the shape it is. As kings and queens, we should be discussing strategies about the new territory we are going to conquer for our King.

The Purpose of Man

Again, I go back to the purpose for which God created man. A man is someone who has a relationship with his heavenly Father, knows his purpose, and has dominion over at least one area of life, not someone who likes to have fun all the time. Toddlers want to play all the time. Unfortunately we have too many toddlers in grown-up bodies. Being born a male is a natural process, but becoming a man is not easy. We have many male humans but very few real men in our society. A woman is someone who is joined to such a man, fulfilling their God-given purpose together. It is very hard to find couple like these today.

Imagine what it must have been like in Eden when God brought Eve to Adam. God never mentioned a thing to Eve. Nothing about submitting to her husband, nothing about bringing up children, and nothing about anything in the garden or the Tree of the Knowledge of Good and Evil. What was God expecting or thinking?

These were two totally free individuals, coming together to become one. When a man and woman are joined and become one, one person does not need to control the other person. God expected them to be led by His Spirit in everything, as free agents. Self-governing is God's idea for individuals. Self-governing means each person is led by the Holy Spirit and produces the fruit of the Spirit. We have mistakenly interpreted this as being independent.

Submission Should Not Be Forced

We are not led by the Spirit as we are supposed to be. That is why we need to be taught about submission, or we try to control the other person. When both individuals are led by the Spirit all the time, then there is no need of forced submission. When God took Eve out of Adam, the same spirit that was in Adam went into Eve. She had the same knowledge and understanding Adam had. God did not breathe into Eve to make her a living soul as He did to Adam.

The best example of this is Jesus and His relationship with His Father. Jesus was completely free as an individual, similar to Adam, but He had no problem submitting to His Father in everything because He was led by the Holy Spirit. Only a person who is spiritually and emotionally bound has a problem with submission. And only a person who is spiritually and emotionally bound tries to control and dominate others.

Because men and women are bound, one tries to control and dominate the other and there is a fight for freedom and liberation. What neither realizes is that they both need deliverance to get back to God's original intent for them. This will only happen if they are free.

When Jesus was questioned by the Pharisees about marriage and divorce, He took them back to the beginning, back to how marriage began.[48] That is the original plan God has for marriage and family, and it is still His plan today. Consider what our culture and media has done to reshape our minds about family and marriage, drawing us away from God's plan and idea.

Kingdom Training Starts with the Family

How do we restore families in order to form a kingdom family? How do we do this practically in today's world? We all need deliverance and healing

---

48 See Matthew 19:4-8.

from the lies and assumptions we hold as true. They are so ingrained in us that we do not even see anything wrong with them. We need to go back to Genesis as Jesus told us. We read the Bible, but it doesn't make any sense to us because of the enemy's strongholds that exist in our mind.

I am sure Adam and Eve, or Abraham and Sarah, did not take their children to an amusement park or throw them in front of a TV screen, or sign them up for a sports team while they were young. But even without those things going on, Cain killed Abel. Imagine what our children are facing in today's culture. That is why the Bible says, "Train up a child in the way he should go, and when he is old he will not depart from it" (Proverbs 22:6).

There is no neutral ground. Everything is under the influence and belongs to and comes from one of the two kingdoms. Either something belongs to the kingdom of God or it belongs to the kingdom of darkness. There is nothing just "cool" and "cute." No, it either belongs to the kingdom of God or the kingdom of Satan. If you look at the garden of Eden, it was very clear. Everything belonged to Adam and Eve, except that one tree. There was no neutral ground. The woman saw the fruit of that tree and said, "Oh, wow, this looks so good, so beautiful, and it will make me wise if I eat it." That is exactly what happens in today's world. We look at the things the devil made, and we are mesmerized by them. Then we bring them into their homes without recognizing which kingdom they come from.

People teach their children, from a very young age, to love the world and things in it. When their children walk away from God as adults, the parents wonder why their children are not walking with God or why they are not passionate for Him. Honey, let me tell you with all my love, you brought things into your home which you thought were "neat" and "cool," and "fun" but they came from the kingdom of darkness. You didn't even know it.

The devil took hold of your children's minds and once they became adults, you saw the fruit of it. That's it. One of the major problems with the church today is that believers do not differentiate what is of God's kingdom and what is not. They do not know what is of the Babylonian system and what is of the kingdom of God. Everything is geared toward having fun. As long as something is fun, it is good. That is the mentality of this generation. It has nothing to do with the kingdom of God. This is called hedonism,[49] the pursuit of pleasure, sensual, self-indulgence; an ethical theory that pleasure (in the sense of the satisfaction of desires) is the highest good and proper aim of human life. Wow!

Today, we see people come to church wearing their favorite sports team's jerseys to show their commitment and solidarity for their team. Would they wear a "Jesus Loves You" jersey when they go to a game? If not, my dear friend, it is time to declare the Lordship of Jesus over your life and renounce every other god and demon to which you have pledged your allegiance and worship. Worship is not singing. What you are the most passionate about is what you worship, and what you worship is your god, believe it or not.

When an unbeliever produces a movie, they are not trying to help you or your children in any way. They have two goals, to make money and to expand the kingdom of their father, the devil (though they may not all be aware of the second). As I said before, there is no neutral ground or neutral person anywhere on earth. There is no place or person that does not belong to either of these two kingdoms operating in the universe. *Everything, everyone, everywhere* either belongs to God or they are under the influence of Satan. Believe me on this one, even if you do not believe anything else I ever said.

Ours is a culture that is deeply engaged in entertainment and having fun. Most people don't realize this is the domain of the kingdom of Satan. Look at the lives of many of the child movie or entertainment stars that

---

49 "hedonism", Google, accessed February 24, 2017, https://www.google.com/webhp?-sourceid=chrome-instant&rlz=1C1JZAP_enUS727US727&ion=1&espv=2&ie=UTF-8#q=hedonism&*.

once were so cute. We brought them (their products) into our homes just for fun and made them part of our family and our children's lives. They grew up together. When these stars become adults, many became totally sold out for the devil. Many become promiscuous, addicted to drugs, or confused about their identity as a male or a female. Our children grew up watching them and are addicted to their movies, songs, and products. If they continue in that way they will walk away from God as well. The fire they once had for God when they were little will die out.

This happens through cartoons as well. There are promiscuous and satanic subliminal messages communicated through cartoons and movies, and the spirits attached to them get transferred into your innocent child's spirit and mind without their knowledge or awareness. These could be rated "G" for audience. Most people don't even notice. Spirits are invisible so you do not see them with your natural eyes when they come to you. Most of the time they come through our thoughts and the imaginary realm. You may not realize it (unless you are walking closely with God and most are not) when an evil spirit comes into you until you are faced with a consequence or see the fruit of it manifest in your life at a later time. This may take years. That spirit will wait for the most opportune time in your child's life and manifest as sickness, danger, immorality, or in some other area of their life.

The next time you are out there in the world and see something "cute" that draws you, discern which kingdom it comes from and who it glorifies before you bring it home to your children. If it does not glorify God, it's not worth spending your hard-earned money and contaminating your spiritual environment at home.

Using Wisdom with the World

You may ask me, "Brother, I have shelves full of these kinds of products that belong to the kingdom of darkness. What should I do with it all?" This is why we have dumpsters and fire pits! The best thing is to burn them. If you cannot burn them, throw them into a dumpster and say good-bye to the devil and his kingdom.

I am not saying you should be paranoid about everything. You need to apply the wisdom of God here. As long as we live in this world, we have to deal with this world. You need to be wise and discerning. Most importantly, be led by the Holy Spirit and not your flesh. These are the children of God.

You may think I am an old-school preacher. No, I am not. I am coming from God's school. I have so much fun with God that I don't need anything that belongs to Satan to make me happy or to have fun. There is joy unspeakable in His presence. His joy is my strength. Most people have not tapped into it because they were programmed from childhood to depend on the other kingdom to have fun and make them happy. People of the other kingdom are always looking to do something to have fun and find joy in their lives. It's time to get free. Consider what David said about what he did to have fun and find joy in his life. Let's make that our testimony as well.

> "You have put gladness in my heart, more than in the season that their grain and wine increased. I will both lie down in peace, and sleep; for You alone, O Lord, make me dwell in safety" (Psalm 4:7-8).

> "You will show me the path of life; in Your presence *is* fullness of joy; at Your right hand *are* pleasures forevermore" (Psalm 16:11).

> "They are abundantly satisfied with the fullness of Your house, and You give them drink from the river of Your pleasures" (Psalm 36:8)

> "Then I will go to the altar of God, to God my exceeding joy" (Psalm 43:4).

Can each of us truly say that God is the exceeding joy of our life?

There is one other thing we should do for pleasure and fun, and that is search and study the work and creation of God. Visit places He created and see the wonders of His hands. If we spent a billion years, we would not finish studying and researching the incredible depth of the works of God.

> "The works of the Lord *are* great, studied by all who have pleasure in them" (Psalm 111:2).

If we depend on anything other than the Lord as the source of our joy, it is sin. We are created to walk with Him and know Him. For a true child of God there is no time to leave the eternal source of joy to do anything of this world for the sake of fun.

> "'Be astonished, O heavens, at this, and be horribly afraid; be very desolate,' says the Lord. 'For My people have committed two evils: they have forsaken Me, the fountain of living waters, *and* hewn themselves cisterns—broken cisterns that can hold no water'" (Jeremiah 2:12-13).

We Have to Be Taught!

Humans are the only species that need to be taught about everything. Other creatures have a natural instinct to do certain things, but humans need to be taught almost everything: how to eat, what to eat, how to walk, how to clean themselves, how to brush their teeth, and so on. When a child reaches five or six years old, he goes to school for the next twelve or fifteen years to learn more.

Just because a baby is born male does not mean he will grow up and know how to be a man, or a husband or a father. It's the same with a female; just because a baby is female doesn't mean she will grow up and know how to be a woman, or a wife and a mother. Each person has to be taught what it means to be a man or a woman. What does it mean to be a husband or a wife? In today's world, everything is based on external factors like how a person looks.

There should be courses in our churches, schools, and universities about manhood and womanhood because most people were not taught these things. Society just expects us to know it all. There is much confusion out there. A man is not sure if he is a man, and a woman is not sure if she is a woman. Men are trying to become women and women are trying to be men. They are trying to define who they are. Unfortunately, most of the knowledge we inherit is from the entertainment world—which is far from any reality.

There is a growing generation in our world today that does not want to be identified as male or female. They might have a particular sexual organ, but they don't know what it means to be a man or woman. They are confused because no one is teaching them about it while they are growing up. The only thing they were taught is how to have fun. Many of them grew up without both parents at home. Today, in our culture, instead of teaching and training our children to be kings and queens, we focus on training them in the things of this world.

The secularists and the women's rights movements are working hard to eliminate gender differences. They are working against the very core of what God established from the beginning. They are the direct representatives of Lucifer and his kingdom.

Instead of teaching our children the most valuable things about life and godliness, they have been trained to follow the notions of their body and to gratify the lust of their flesh and eyes, without ever being accountable for the consequences of their actions.

That is why the Bible says woe to a land when their king is a child. What does that mean? What does a child like to do? A child likes to play and have fun. It also refers to a king who is not mature. Unfortunately, many kings these days sacrifice their purpose and dominion for the sake of having fun.

"Woe to you, O land, when your **king** *is* a child, and your princes feast in the morning!" (Ecclesiastes 10:16).

A king should not love pleasure.

"A **ruler** who lacks understanding *is* a great oppressor, *but* he who hates covetousness will prolong *his* days" (Proverbs 28:16).

Prosperity teaching has deceived the saints about their purpose because it has focused so much on money and making money. And while we were all busy trying to make money, the devil came in through the back door and stole our nation, marriage, and children from us.

Kingdom Culture

Every nation and kingdom has a culture. When you were born you became a citizen of a country, and when you were born again you became a citizen of another country called the kingdom of heaven. From that very moment, it became your responsibility to learn how this new country or kingdom operated. That is why Jesus said, "Seek first the kingdom of God and His righteousness and all these things shall be added unto you" (Matthew 6:33). He did not say to seek Him first, but His kingdom. There are two ways to meet your basic needs on earth. One is to depend on the system of the natural country you are living in, or learn how the kingdom of God operates: and everything you ever need will be added to you.

Jesus introduced His kingdom in Matthew 4:17 and told people to repent. In Matthew 5 to 7, He introduced the culture and decrees and laws of His kingdom, or how the citizens in His kingdom should think and act. Please read those chapters to find out the culture of the kingdom of God.

The church worldwide is plagued by racism and the caste system. People bring their culture in with them when they come to church, without knowing that when they were born again they renounced their citizenship from the country of their natural birth and became a citizen of a new kingdom. In the new kingdom, every human being from every race, language, and color, is a child of the same Father, and citizens of the same kingdom. There is no division or superiority based on color or caste.

Kingdom Decrees and Laws

In a kingdom, whatever the king decrees becomes the law of the land. A kingdom is not governed by a constitution legislated by the majority or by the people. The king decides what the law of the land should be.

When Jesus began His public ministry after announcing His kingdom in Matthew 4:17, He decreed the laws and culture of His kingdom. These laws are not limited to those chapters in Matthew, but they are the foundation of His kingdom.

"Righteousness delivers from death" (Proverbs 10:2b). There is still a place for righteousness in our life. We are the righteousness of God by faith in Christ Jesus. As children of God we are required to be righteous in all our endeavors.

> "Blessings *are* on the head of the righteous, but violence covers the mouth of the wicked" (Proverbs 10:6).

Chapter 6

Administering the Kingdom of God, Part 2

"Oh, let the nations be glad and sing for joy! For You shall judge the people righteously, And govern the nations on earth"
(Psalm 67:4).

Kingdom Army

In the early church, every believer was a soldier and the apostles were like generals in the army. This was a different kind of army. They did not fight with swords and spears, but they had authority over all other kingdoms and kings in the natural and in the spirit, e.g., when the apostles were arrested and put in prison by the rulers of a natural kingdom, the *ekklesia* prayed and cancelled the rule and authority of those kingdoms and governments.

One of the names of our God is the Lord of hosts. He is the Captain of the army. He has a host of angels that do His battle. No one can fight like our God and none can defeat Him. He is the King of glory, the Lord strong and mighty. He is mighty in battle (Psalm 24:8-10).

> "The Portion of Jacob *is* not like them, for He *is* the Maker of all things; and *Israel is* the tribe of His inheritance. The Lord of hosts *is* His name. You *are* My battle-ax *and* weapons of war: for with you I will break the nation in pieces; with you I will destroy kingdoms" (Jeremiah 51:19-20).

Kingdom Education

The education system today teaches people many things they will never use or need in life, but it does not teach the essential things a person must know, such as discovering their purpose, helping people find their gifts, family life, managing money and talents, and so on. In fact, almost everything taught is anti-God. The body of Christ needs to come up with the best educational programs. God intended for those programs to be done through the church. In every nation and city the church should run the best schools, colleges, and universities.

Each of you is a solution to a problem that exists on this earth today. Maybe not the whole earth, but at least in your community or to an individual. Each one of us is anointed to set free a part of creation from bondage. All creation came under bondage because of Adam's disobedience, but Jesus died to pay for our sins and to set us free from bondage. Now it's our job to set creation free from its bondage.

As was stated in chapter one, statistics show that less than 1% of the world's population knows their purpose.

We Have the Solution!

Jesus said that we are the light of the world. Light is the solution for darkness. The church is supposed to be the solution to the darkness that is in this world. Instead, we look to the world for solutions to our problems. What a pathetic situation!

Chapter 6| Administering the Kingdom of God, Part 2

There is one agency God put on this earth that should be able to provide solutions to the problems our world is facing. There is one body that should have the answers to the age-old questions every generation asks. There is one group of people that should represent the Lord God Almighty to the rest of creation. That is us: the church.

We should be helping people discover their purpose. There is no population problem, only a purpose problem. There is no poverty problem, only a productivity problem. There are too many people who are not productive. The number one reason is because they do not understand their purpose.

Kingdom education is not based on getting a college degree. Kingdom education is discovering your purpose first; and then if necessary, finding the right college degree to receive the training that will help you fulfill that purpose. Many people grow up with the concept of going to school and then to a college to get a degree and find a job. That's the way our culture programmed us and that is the world's way of living. As kingdom citizens, we are not supposed to base our lives on the world's system. First, discover your purpose, and then find the right education that will help you fulfill that purpose.

The tragedy is that the majority of the people who are alive on this earth today do not know their purpose. The reason population is a problem in many countries is because the majority of the people do not know what to do with their lives so they either demand the government take care of them or try to steal from others. Many people remain poor because they do not produce anything. When those two problems are solved (population and productivity), we will see any nation's economy being transformed.

Once you decide what you want to do with your life, you need to get the education that helps you fulfill that purpose. I have seen many precious people go to colleges and universities to earn degrees, but later find they are called to do something entirely different than what they learned. They wasted money and their precious time doing that.

Spirit-focused Education

Kingdom education is different from worldly education. Kingdom education is focused on developing your God-given talents and abilities (which are in seed form) to influence the world. It is focused on your spirit. It is focused on gaining wisdom. Without wisdom there is no foundation and no real education.

In the world today, we see so many "educated people" who have degrees from prestigious universities, but they lack basic wisdom. They do not even understand the basic differences between humans and animals, male and female. They regard both in the same category. This is because their spirit has not received any education. Their mind has knowledge but they did not acknowledge God, so He gave them up to become reprobate in their minds.[50]

When we read the Bible, we see that God founded the earth by wisdom and established the heavens by understanding.[51] A house also needs to be founded on wisdom and understanding.[52] When we read about Jesus, we see that He grew in wisdom and stature.[53] We do not read that He was enrolled in the Roman school system and was the best student. No. His life was founded on wisdom; even the Pharisees were amazed at His teaching.

The majority of Christians are following the world system but do not even have as much wisdom and understanding as the world about how it operates. When a person is educated, he knows that area of study. When you master a talent, ability, skill, profession, subject, or a trade, you become educated in that area. You subdue and take dominion over it. You are ready to rule over that area and have a following.

---

50 See Romans 1:28.

51 See Proverbs 3:19.

52 See Proverbs 24:3.

53 See Luke 2:52.

Chapter 6 | Administering the Kingdom of God, Part 2

You do not always need to go to a college or university to be educated. Many times, those who do are not truly educated because they know a little bit about many things but master nothing. Being educated does not mean you graduate from a university with a certificate. There are people who have never been to school but have mastered an art or ability and make a much better living than college graduates. Some of the inventors and great entrepreneurs of our time dropped out of school or college, but they became famous because they mastered an area of life like no one else ever had before. In the spirit and in the natural, they became famous because they mastered one area of knowledge, trade, technology, a talent, or an idea, and went with it. Anyone can do it; it's not a secret. People like Moses, Joseph, Thomas Edison, Orville and Wilbur Wright, Bill Gates, Steve Jobs, and the list goes on. They mastered their purpose and succeeded.

That is the premise of kingdom education. There are many auto mechanics in India who have never been to school, but they mastered their trade by practicing it and watching others. That is discipleship. They joined the workshop as an apprentice and learned the job by doing it. Some of the best hairdressers that I know in India never went to school either, not even grade school.

When we look at the people in the Bible that God used, we see the same pattern. God's anointing gives you the ability to master an area of life. God's examples in the Bible learned the ways of God through life experience. The Bible says John the Baptist was in the wilderness until he revealed himself to Israel. What was he doing in the wilderness? The Bible says He grew strong in spirit.[54] He may not have known arithmetic, but he focused on what he needed to fulfill his purpose and mastered it, which was to become strong in spirit.

The Bible says John the Baptist was the Elijah that was to come. He came in the spirit of Elijah, but he performed no signs or miracles[55] Why

---

54 See Luke 1:80.

55 See John 10:41.

not? Usually, we associate Elijah with his miracles (like bringing fire from heaven) and we sing songs like, "These are the days of Elijah." The spirit of Elijah manifests differently in each generation. In John, it manifested as a bridge between two dispensations (the Law and grace). It turned the spiritual tide (atmosphere) of this earth into a new era of grace. He was the forerunner of Jesus Christ. He gave birth to a new season in the Spirit. If his spirit were to manifest now, it would be different than anything we saw in the Bible. May the Lord open our eyes to see what His Spirit is doing today!

Purpose Revolution Centers

The Holy Spirit put a vision in my heart to start Purpose Revolution Centers in every nation. These are storefronts where anyone can come to discover their purpose. They will fill out a questionnaire that helps them pinpoint their passion, talents, and gifts. The ultimate goal of these places will be to help people get connected with their Creator, because only the manufacturer knows the purpose of a product.

I am in the process of developing the materials. It is a huge task and will take more than one person to do it. If you are inspired by God to be part of it, please let me know. I want to form a team of like-minded people. This may be the second largest problem next to sin that humanity has—and the church is supposed to solve it. Jesus solved the sin problem.

Kingdom Economy

It is common for us to think when we hear the word economy as cash, stocks, savings, business or any other money-making methods. These things are part of the world's economy. Kingdom economy runs on a different system and is based on the wealth God has created. It is not based on money or a credit system as we think about economy today. It is depended up on things that *create* money. As long as the kingdom of God remains it's economy also will remain. This world's economy depends on the economy of the kingdom.

Kingdom economy starts with land. Everything that controls the economy of a nation comes from the land. In any country, people who own land have influence and wealth. The more land you own, the more influence you have. Just because you own land does not mean you have money. You need to utilize that land to produce something that will create the money you need.

Some of the ideas were already mentioned, but let's recap a few of them. First, the early church had a banking system to meet the needs of its members. Second, many of them sold a portion of their assets, and brought the money to the apostles. The apostles distributed that money so that every need was met. This is a picture of kingdom living.

> "Now the multitude of those who believed were of one heart and one soul; neither did anyone say that any of the things he possessed was his own, but they had all things in common. And with great power the apostles gave witness to the resurrection of the Lord Jesus. And great grace was upon them all. Nor was there anyone among them who lacked; for all who were possessors of lands or houses sold them, and brought the proceeds of the things that were sold, and laid *them* at the apostles' feet; and they distributed to each as anyone had need" (Acts 4:32-35).

Third, not everyone sold all they had, or they could not have gone from house to house every day.

> "Now all who believed were together, and had all things in common, and sold their possessions and goods, and divided them among all, as anyone had need. So continuing daily with one accord in the temple, and breaking bread from house to house, they ate their food with gladness and simplicity of heart" (Acts 2:44-46).

> "And daily in the temple, and in every house, they did not cease teaching and preaching Jesus *as* the Christ" (Acts 5:42).

Many in the church today believe that if they tithe regularly, one day they will be financially free and wealthy. According to the Bible, that is not true. The Bible never teaches that if you pay tithes you will be financially wealthy, though in the Bible, financially wealthy people paid tithes. The best example is the father of our faith, Abraham, who began the principle of tithing. He was a rich man way before he ever gave any tithe. There is also no evidence that shows Abraham paid a tithe regularly. We read about the one-time encounter he had with Melchizedek, the king of Salem to whom he gave a tithe.

God said in Deuteronomy 8:18: "And you shall remember the Lord your God, for *it is* He who gives you power to get wealth, that He may establish His covenant which He swore to your fathers, as *it is* this day."

There is no "one size fits all" financial principle in the Bible. God worked differently with different people in different times and cultures.

There is a power of God available to create wealth. God understands better than we do that it requires wealth to establish His covenant. He has made His power available to His children to create wealth. We need to learn to tap into that power. God has anointed many with this ability, but they do not know how to put it to work.

God has blessed us with all we need. Those things exist either in the invisible spirit realm or in the hands of the wicked. How do we bring them from the invisible to the visible?

The Wealth of the Wicked

> "A good man leaves an inheritance to his children's children, but the wealth of the sinner is stored up for the righteous" (Proverbs 13:22).

I have seen many claim this verse without understanding what it really means or how it works. When you see the wealth of the wicked, you cannot simply take it for yourself. Nor are the wicked going to bring their wealth and leave it at your doorstep. There is very little chance of it happening that way. We need the wisdom of God to know how to bring the wealth of the wicked into the kingdom.

Instead we must possess it. Just because God said He has given you something does not mean you possess it. The Lord told the Israelites that He had given them the Promised Land, but it wasn't theirs until they possessed it. They had to fight to inherit the promises of God.

How do we fight to possess the wealth of the wicked? There are three ways you possess the wealth of the wicked.

1) Businesses/Products

When you come up with a valid product that is good for humanity you are creating a legitimate path to tap into the wealth of the wicked. When you have a product, people will trade money to buy that product. The better and more useful the product, the more people will by it. Each time someone buys your product you are inheriting a some of the wealth of the wicked.

2) Services

When you offer a service that people need for which you are paid. If you own a telephone company and you have many subscribers, they pay you for using your service. If you cut and style hair and own a barber shop, you are paid for that. Everyone needs a haircut at some point in their life. If you are a dentist and provide that service to the people in your community, you will be blessed through that service. When you provide a service that people need, you will inherit the wealth of the wicked and build relationships at the same time.

3) Favor

The third way the wealth of the wicked is transferred to you is through God giving you favor. It's happened many times in history, but may not happen to everyone. If you are supposed to start a business, you are not going to receive wealth through favor, but through the business God is leading you to develop. God gave the people of Israel favor with the Egyptians and they plundered them of all their valuables. Another example is Nehemiah. He received the resources he needed from the king to go back to Jerusalem and rebuild its walls.

Supernatural Millionaires

When you read the Bible, you notice something powerful and very important in relation to ministers and believers and their financial life. In the Bible, ministers like Elijah and Elisha and Paul made others rich by supernatural means. There is an anointing God is releasing upon the body of Christ to become millionaires.

How do you supernaturally create millionaires? The secret is revealed in the Bible. You can go from rags to riches overnight when the supernatural power of God works in your life to create wealth. God said that it is He who gives power to create wealth. He loves to transfer money into your account and meet all your needs so you can become a blessing to someone else.

There are several incidents in the Bible where God's people went from being broke to becoming rich in a matter of hours. This grace of God is available for you to become wealthy. You have to believe it in order for this to manifest in your life. God wants to raise up super-wealthy believers in different nations to establish His covenant in those countries. You cannot remain poor and establish God's covenant.

How did Adam and Abraham become wealthy? Adam received the entire earth from God his Father as an inheritance. He owned all of the wealth that existed on the earth. God told Him about gold and precious stones. That's real wealth, and it is one of the foundations of kingdom economy.[56]

God called Abraham in Genesis 12. In Genesis 13 we see a wealthy Abraham. How did he become so rich in cattle, gold and silver, and servants? It was supernatural. Kings donated resources to him. The land was overwhelmingly being filled by their wealth.

When the Israelites came out of Egypt, they came out with great riches. God told them to ask their neighbors for precious jewels and clothes, and they plundered the Egyptians. They were abused and misused for almost four hundred years. They didn't know what they were missing until the day of redemption came. Today, there are millions of believers who are not aware of what really belongs to them.

We see many people in the Bible who became supernaturally wealthy overnight: Joseph, David, the widows in Elijah's and Elisha's time, Esther, Ruth, all of the people of Israel. These are only some of the examples. This supernatural grace is still available in the kingdom of God to those who believe.

Spiritual Inheritance

Here's another secret I found in Scripture: The responsibility of a truly anointed servant of God is to cause others to possess what really belongs to them in the spirit. Moses and Joshua took the entire people of Israel to help them possess their spiritual inheritance. We need ministers like that in our day. Unfortunately, many ministers steal from their people instead of empowering them. These are not true minsters of the gospel. They are wolves in sheep's clothing. A true minister of the gospel will empower others to tap into their spiritual inheritance for the benefit of the kingdom, and is not focused on personal gain. Paul said that he has made many rich.

---

56 See Genesis 2:8-14.

If you study the lives of these people you will see they have something in common. Their intention was to help others to discover and fulfill their purpose. This is why Abraham gave Lot the first choice of the land and where he wanted to live when they were forced to separate. Abraham had the grace of God upon him to turn a desert into a garden, and Lot didn't. Moses, Elijah, and Elisha also created instant millionaires by supernatural grace.

Elijah and Elisha helped start businesses. When the widow's oil was multiplied, it was an instant miracle of supernatural wealth. She went from being poor to wealthy in a matter of a few hours. In all of these instances, those involved had to do something. It was not free money transferred into their account. They were given a business idea or an opportunity, which they had to put to work and develop.

The church in Corinth was a very special church. Though they had many moral issues, they were one of the most powerful churches in the Spirit that Paul established. He said they became instantly wealthy. They began to reign in life. That is what God intends for every church in every nation.

Paul said that even though he seemed to be poor in the natural, he possessed all things. That means He had the power to release anything to anyone at any time. This is true apostolic grace and authority. Paul could make a person rich instantly.[57]

The best example of all is our Lord Jesus. He became poor for our sake, so that through His poverty we can become rich.[58] Why did the Creator of the universe and the greatest King of all time choose to be born poor on this earth? It was not an accident but a deliberate choice for the sake of many who were stuck under the curse of poverty.

---

57 See 2 Corinthians 6:10.

58 See 2 Corinthians 8:9.

The saddest thing that happened with the modern prosperity movement is that instead of empowering believers to become what God created them to be, many ministers empowered themselves and took advantage of ignorant believers and became wealthy, while the majority of the believers remained living hand-to-mouth or in survival mode.

If these ministers had empowered believers to become wealthy by starting businesses and engaging in local politics, the United States wouldn't be in the shape it is in now. We would have had a different outcome. I believe with all my heart that it is not too late to start over.

Treasures of Wickedness Profit Nothing

Proverbs 10:2 tells us that treasures or wealth accumulated through wickedness do not profit anything. Most people are trying to make money to survive. They will do that through any means, including lying, cheating, stealing, and more. I recently read a news article about the biggest ATM theft in history.

It happened in Japan. Japanese police were investigating a nationwide ATM heist after nearly £8.8 million, or 1.4 billion yen (¥), was illegally withdrawn from 1,400 cash machines in the span of two hours. Cash was withdrawn almost simultaneously across Tokyo and sixteen other prefectures using as many as 1,600 counterfeit credit cards containing account information stolen from the South African institution Standard Bank!

This is just one example of people obtaining treasures of wickedness.

> "He who has a slack hand becomes poor, but the hand of the diligent makes rich" (Proverbs 10:4).

This verse reveals one of the secrets to why some people remain poor and others become rich. He who has a slack hand becomes poor. You can sit and complain about your poverty and your misfortune all day long. That is not going to change anything. It will only lead to more poverty.

This verse describes two types of hands: the slack hand and the diligent hand. It tells us that poverty and riches depend on the hands of people. "Hands" denotes what we do with our life, our work. Some people are born without hands. Others find it hard to move their hand to do anything. They will find an excuse for everything. In the morning they will say it's too early and they will do it in the evening. When the evening comes, they will postpone it to the next day because it's too late. Months and years go by and they never accomplish anything. Having a slack hand does not mean they are not doing anything. Slack hands can be busy or seem busier than productive people, but they have no goals and therefore produce no fruit. They lack discipline and diligence.

> "He who gathers in summer *is* a wise son; he who sleeps
> in harvest *is* a son who causes shame" (Proverbs 10:5).

Summer has different meanings in the Bible. It means the hot season in the natural. But it also means the prime of our life. There is a season in each person's life in which they need to be working hard. If they miss that season it will be very difficult to catch up later. "He who gathers in summer" is a picture of someone who saves and invests in the prime of life. They will be safe when he or she gets old or when hard times come.

The Foundations of Kingdom Economy

God mentioned the foundations of kingdom economy in Genesis. They consist of five things: wisdom, land, agriculture, precious metals and stones, and water. As long as these remain, God's kingdom economy on earth will never experience any recession or economic collapse.

1. Wisdom

There is something on this earth that is more costly than silver and gold.

> "Happy *is* the man *who* finds wisdom, and the man *who*
> gains understanding; for her proceeds *are* better than

the profits of silver, and her gain than fine gold. She *is* more
precious than rubies, and all the things you may desire
cannot compare with her" (Proverbs 3:13-15).

There is something more powerful than weapons of war.

"Wisdom *is* better than weapons of war" (Ecclesiastes 9:18a).

There is something that is harder to find than any hidden treasure. There is something that everyone seeks and only a few find. There is something that is better than strength.

"Wisdom *is* better than strength" (Ecclesiastes 9:16a).

It is wisdom. That is the number one foundation of kingdom economy. Before God created the earth and all its wealth, He created wisdom. Then He used wisdom to create everything else.

"The Lord by wisdom founded the earth; by understanding He established the heavens" (Proverbs 3:19).

The Bible says wisdom has two hands. Everything we look and work for with our life, we will find if we have wisdom.

"Length of days *is* in her right hand, in her left hand riches and honor" (Proverbs 3:16).

God tells us to seek wisdom and find understanding before we seek any material blessings.

"Wisdom *is* the principal thing; *therefore* get wisdom. And in all your getting, get understanding" (Proverbs 4:7).

Wisdom is the most expensive thing. God said His people perish for only one thing: That is the lack of knowledge (Hosea 4:6). The foundation of everything we do must be wisdom, whether it is marriage, business, or any other relationship, it must be established on wisdom.

The Bible says a house is built by wisdom and by knowledge its rooms are filled with precious treasures (Proverbs 24:3-4).

Everything God does is grounded in sound wisdom. Before He releases His power to a person, or a situation, He will make sure His wisdom precedes it.

That is why the Bible says Jesus increased in wisdom and stature before the power of God came upon Him (Luke 2:52).

On the first day God created light, but He created the sun, moon, and stars only on the fourth day. What was the light He created on the first day? It was wisdom. He separated light from darkness, knowledge from ignorance.

Before we set out to build a business or make money, the first thing we need to gain is wisdom. The root cause of every problem we face in life is because of ignorance.

2. Land

The second foundation of a kingdom's economy is based on how much land a kingdom occupies. In a nutshell, the size of a kingdom is determined by how much land it possesses. In Esther we read that the Persian kingdom of King Ahasuerus extended from Ethiopia to India.[59] It was one of the most powerful kingdoms that ever existed on the face of the earth. Land is the chief foundation of a kingdom and its economy. When God began His kingdom here, the entire earth was the territory of His kingdom. He gave that to His children to manage. The Bible begins by saying, "In the beginning God created the heavens and the earth" (Genesis 1:1). Heaven is His throne and earth is His footstool. If heaven is only His throne and the planet Earth is only big enough to be His footstool, imagine the size of His kingdom. It's beyond human comprehension. I read that scientists

---

59 See Esther 1:1.

have discovered that the universe is big enough to hold millions of solar systems like ours.

Why is land the chief foundation of the economy of a kingdom or a nation? Because everything we use for our survival comes out of the land. Every product, our food, water, clothing, everything imaginable is a product of the land. That is why God began in Genesis with the land.

> "Moreover the profit of the land is for all; *even* the king is served from the field" (Ecclesiastes 5:9).

Before He introduced His power, gifts, or any other thing, He wants us to know about the relationship He has with the land. It is interesting to note that God calls the land His land[60] just like He calls people His people.[61] We need to call the land our land.

In nations where the people are poor, they do not love the land God gave them. They do not take care of the land, and they do not appreciate or cultivate it. They think land is a waste and has no value. They sell it to others cheaply and think the cash they receive from the sale will make them rich. It's just the opposite; they will end up poorer later than they were before. Land is the most expensive commodity you can possess. If you do not value the land, it is because you have no idea about real wealth and what it can produce for you.

If you look at the land in poor countries, it is usually unkempt and disorderly and dirty. They have no system to take care of garbage and the land is covered with filth. They are always looking for something for free. That is what lazy and ignorant people do. If you look at the richer countries, the land is treated with respect and kept neat and orderly. I have come to the conclusion that the main difference between poor and rich countries is how they care for their land. In poor countries patriotism (love for their nation) is also very minimal. Most are trying to get out of their country to

---

60 See Joel 2:18 and Zechariah 9:16.

61 See Psalm 100:3.

find a better living somewhere else. On the other hand, in rich countries patriotism is a heartfelt attitude.

> "Much food *is in* the fallow *ground* of the poor" (Proverbs 13:23a).

> "He who tills his land will have plenty of bread, but he who follows frivolity will have poverty enough!" (Proverbs 28:19).

Proverbs 24:30-34 says:

> "I went by the field of the lazy *man*,
> And by the vineyard of the man devoid of understanding;

> "And there it was, all overgrown with thorns;
> Its surface was covered with nettles;
> Its stone wall was broken down.

> "When I saw *it,* I considered *it* well;
> I looked on *it and* received instruction:

> "A little sleep, a little slumber,
> A little folding of the hands to rest;

> "So shall your poverty come *like* a prowler,
> And your need like an armed man."

In most parts of the world, a person who owns the most land has more influence than others. Your purpose is connected to your land. If you study the Bible, you will see a pattern that when God favors a people, He gives them land; and when they disobey Him, they lose their land and go into captivity. I was surprised to read that God even went to the extent of telling the people of Israel that if they disobeyed Him, they would lose the land He gave them. And they did.

Does God love the land more than He loves people? There are only two permanent things on this earth: one is our spirit and the second is land.

God cares for the land so much that He protects and fights for it. Every true believer in Christ should ask God for forgiveness for not taking care of the land He gave us and not loving it as much as He loves it.

I was really surprised by a verse I found about the land. The last part says God will destroy those who destroy the earth. It is found in Revelation 11:18, which says, "The nations were angry, and Your wrath has come, and the time of the dead, that they should be judged, and that You should reward Your servants the prophets and the saints, and those who fear Your name, small and great, and should destroy those who destroy the earth."

3. Agriculture

The third foundation of kingdom economy is agriculture. The work God gave to the first human being was to be an agriculturist. In Genesis we read that God created Adam, made a garden for him, and He put the man in it. There are two major expenses in life: the first is land, which includes your house (whether you own or rent), and the second is the food you eat. In any country their economy is depended on its land and agriculture.

4. Precious Metals and Stones

The fourth foundation of kingdom economy is precious metals and stones.[62] Every precious stone and metal that is on this planet belongs to our God and His children. But the enemy stole most of it from us and is hiding it. He is using these to build his kingdom. God explained to Adam:

> "Now a river went out of Eden to water the garden, and from there it parted and became four riverheads. The name of the first *is* Pishon; it *is* the one which skirts the whole land of Havilah, where *there is* gold. And the gold of that land *is* good. Bdellium and the onyx stone *are* there" (Genesis 2:10-12).

---

62 See Genesis 2:12-13.

Why would God tell us in Genesis that the gold and precious stones in one part of the world are good? Because He is teaching us about kingdom economy. He repeatedly said in His Word that all of the gold and silver belong to Him.

> "Because you have taken My silver and My gold, and have carried into your temples My prized possessions" (Joel 3:5).

> "'The silver *is* Mine, and the gold *is* Mine,' says the Lord of hosts" (Haggai 2:8).

When the New Jerusalem comes down from heaven, which we read about in Revelation, its foundation, wall, and gates are made from twelve precious stones, pearls, and pure gold.[63] Why would God give us the details of what is in the land of Gihon, including its gold and precious stones? There are no unnecessary details in the Bible. God does not waste words. If He says something, there is a reason for it. The foundation of any nation's economy depends on how much land they own, what is in that land, and what they do with it. From that comes the amount and quality of food they produce with the resources they extract from the land.

Most people believe and most preachers preach that Lucifer was in charge of worship in heaven. But if you really study the Bible, you will see that he was not just a worshiper. He owned vast amounts of wealth in God's kingdom. He was in charge of the economy, business, trade, wealth, and manufacturing in God's kingdom. He knew God better than all of us combined because he saw Him with his own eyes and experienced Him firsthand. Most of us haven't seen Him. We believe that He exists but lack substantial experience to prove anything.

For the devil that is not the case. He knows how God functions and how His kingdom operates. He copied it well and enabled his children to manifest a counterfeit of it on earth, all the while deceiving God's children because most of us have no idea how God's kingdom operates.

---

63 See Revelation 21:18-21.

Recently I heard the story about a country in the African continent that sold their copper mining rights to an outside company for 25 million US Dollars because they did not have the proper technology. This company came in and made $75 million US Dollars within the first three months of their operation. That is just one example of how precious stones and metals can change the economy of a nation.

5. Water

Water is one of the most precious commodities we have. We cannot live without water. It is also a billion-dollar industry. In 2016 water surpassed carbonated soft drinks as the number one drinking beverage in the US. When God began the restoration of planet Earth in Genesis 1, He gathered all the water into one place and called it the sea. There are many types of wealth in the ocean: oil, fish, minerals, and pearls are just some of them.

In some parts of the United States, when you buy a piece of land you do not own the water rights to that land. That means you cannot dig water out of the land you own. Someone living in a different town or state might own the water rights of the land you own. This was a big surprise to me because in India when you buy a piece of land, you own the water rights too. You can dig a well and use the water for your personal use.

As long as we live on this earth we need water. In Genesis, God taught Adam about the rivers that started in the garden. They were their water sources. God knows water is vital to our life. One of the fastest growing businesses in many parts of the world these days is turning sea water into drinking water.

How to Create Money

Did you know that you can create money? Money is a medium of exchange, something you can exchange for something else of value. If you make something that has a value of ten dollars, you have just created ten dollars. When you exchange that product, idea, information, skill, entertainment, or whatever it is, to someone who needs it, they will pay you ten dollars. It could be anything. Your financial provision is connected to one or more of the following principles, which will generate income to your life. Your purpose will encompass at least one of these areas.

Have a Product

At any given time we might be using at least ten (the number might vary between men and women) kinds of products, made by different companies, on our bodies alone. We paid money to buy them. We use hundreds of products in our homes. Someone made those products and they made money when we bought them!

You might be a person in whom God has deposited a product. The product does not have to be something like an airplane; it could be as small as a paper clip or a rubber band. Not everyone is created to produce a product, so if you do not have a product, there is no need to worry about it. You may be called to help someone who manufactures products instead.

There are many roles you can play in the process of making a product. The first is design. Every product needs a designer to design it. The next role is the manufacturer. You could start a company that manufactures products for others. Another is packaging. There are companies that specialize in making packaging materials. There is also marketing. A product will go nowhere if it is not marketed. Some others are distribution, transportation, and advertising. You could provide the raw materials, or any form of services or tools, to any of the above areas. All of these services generate money, and the people who do these become blessed financially.

Meet a Need

The second way money will come to you is when you meet a need. There are needs all around us. In our nation, church, and community, there are needs waiting to be met. When you meet a particular need, you will be blessed financially. Food meets the need of hunger. Watches solve a time-telling problem. The possibilities are endless.

Serve a Cause

There are causes that are worth committing your life to serve. There are many social and charitable organizations around the world, and they all serve a cause. Our ministry had a Vision Center in India where we trained orphans and destitute children to discover and fulfill their purpose. It's been one of the best programs we ever did as a ministry, to see children who never had any opportunity to go to school, become entrepreneurs, learn skills, and become who God created them to be. Everyone who has come to visit has said they have never seen a program like ours anywhere else. This is just one example.

God will guide you and help you discover such a cause if this is the direction He wishes you to go. Even if you cannot establish a cause, you can support those He touches your heart to serve.

Solve a Problem

You are created to solve a problem. Jesus solved the sin problem. Bill Gates solved a computer problem. Ford solved the automobile problem. Clothes solve the nakedness problem. Whatever problem grieves your heart and makes you cry, you might be created to solve. Every business out there solves a problem, and people pay money when that problem is solved for them.

Add Value to Others

When you add value to others through your wisdom, service, teaching, companionship, however God uses you, you will in turn be blessed, financially and otherwise.

Chapter 7

Administering the Kingdom of God, Part 3

"Why should the nations say, "Where is their God?"
(Psalm 79:10a).

Kingdom Business and Manufacturing

Jesus is the Creator of the universe. Everything you see, and even what you cannot see with your eyes, was created by Jesus. How do we witness Jesus as the Creator?

> *"All things were made through Him,* and without Him nothing was made that was made" (John 1:3).

> *"For by Him all things were created* that are in heaven and that are on earth, visible and invisible" (Colossians 1:16).

> "And to make all see what *is* the fellowship of the mystery, which from the beginning of the ages has been hidden in *God who created* all things through Jesus Christ" (Ephesians 3:9).

God introduces Himself in the Bible as the Creator first in Genesis 1:1. The root of all our problems is that we do not pay attention to Genesis, to see how everything began. If we do not know how everything began and why it began, we won't understand the reason for our existence. Confusion and chaos are the result, as we see around us.

Why does God introduce Himself as the Creator first before He reveals Himself as Healer, Prophet, or King? As His children, that is the *first* attribute He wants us to imitate. For some reason, we have ignored that for a long time, and gave this work over to the devil and his children. The devil knows more about God than most Christians. He copies God in almost everything He does, but we are the ones who are supposed to do that.

Everything God created has the potential to be an idea for business. From the tiniest atom to the tallest mountain, snow to the mosquitoes, all were created for man to make businesses. Thousands of families make a living from the snow. People make pest control businesses out of mosquitoes and spiders. Training people to climb Mount Everest is a business in India and Nepal. The sun, moon, wind, and seawater can businesses. All the food that we eat that comes from plants is produced by sunlight. Solar panels and other energy-producing methods depend on the heat from the sun, light, or wind.

We are surrounded by products and raw materials created by God. We need to use our creativity to use the raw materials to produce something and make a business out of it. That is why when Jesus shared the parable of the talents (or minas). It says the nobleman gave minas to all of his servants and told them, "Do business till I come" (Luke 19:13b). We should be training God's children to excel in business.

We Are to Be Fruitful

We depend on various products for our sustenance, and they all come from the earth. The first commandment God gave to man was to be fruitful. We are created in three parts: spirit, soul, and body. He wants us to be fruitful in each of those areas. The fruit of our body can be our children and the works of our hands. The fruit of our mind could be inventions, products, and ideas. The fruit of our spirit is love, joy, peace, and so on as well as our spiritual children.

Every product you use is the fruit of a person's mind or imagination. Most people do not use their mind for anything productive or creative. There are two groups of people in this world, producers and consumers. Producers make decisions for the consumers. The church is supposed to be the most productive of all agencies, but we became the most consuming instead. This has to change.

When I am in church, I look around and see people with great potential. The problem is that they have not used even a small portion of that potential. They are all waiting for something: for God to show up or for the rapture. What a sad dilemma. I wonder what God thinks about this up in heaven. I am sure He is grieved.

The church has been conditioned by the religious spirit from a young age, robbed of their inheritance and the potential God their Father, gave them. They are afraid of what is going to happen to their lives and are trying to survive. We sing in church about how great our God is with nothing to show His greatness or creativity. We need to throw out our religiosity and this handicapped mentality and come alive as sons and daughters of the Almighty God: as kings and queens.

I am writing all of this to stir us up. We need to start training at least our future generations to do things differently and correctly; to take their rightful place and release the potential God put in them. They should not wait around for rapture or revival when God has given and done for us everything we ever needed. We should not let their minds be programmed with movies and sports. We should program their minds as kings and queens. As I said earlier, the first Scripture every human being should learn in their life is Genesis 1:26, which explains the very purpose of our existence. If you miss that, you miss everything else.

Products Equal Influence

People with products have influence. Governments of this world, for the most part, are influenced or controlled by people in business. How do we witness that Jesus is the Creator in these areas? The church needs to come up with products that are useful for the people in the world.

The majority of our money is spent on products and services. God did not create airplanes, but He created the raw materials necessary to make them and hid them in the earth. God did not create furniture, but He created trees and gave us a brain to imagine and create what we needed from them. God did not create automobiles, but He created everything we needed to make one. It's up to us to use our imagination to make what we need. God gave us the earth, but we have not used it the best way. We have not cared for it well either. Unfortunately, we have been waiting to get out of our planet. What a sad dilemma!

In most countries, key companies have more influence than the worldwide church combined. What if those companies were run by believers? It is time for the church to reclaim lost territories and emerge as innovators like our Lord Jesus Christ. The Holy Spirit is the Architect of the universe in which we exist, and Earth is just one tiny planet in that universe. I once read that the sun can contain 1.3 million earth-sized planets.[64] It is time to take the Holy Spirit out of the box we put Him in. We thought He came just to heal the sick, help us speak in tongues, and give us emotional experiences. We were wrong.

Products Help Solve Problems

Many people turn their brains off when they become born again. We need to use our brains to come up with products and services that are helpful to humanity and become valuable to our society—not a nuisance! We need to open our minds and become productive and creative.

---

64 Fraser Cain, "How Many Earths Can Fit in the Sun?" Universe Today, December 24, 2015, accessed February 16, 2017, http://www.universetoday.com/65356/how-many-earths-can-fit-in-the-sun.

Chapter 7 | Administering the Kingdom of God, Part 3

All the treasures of wisdom and knowledge are hid in Christ (Colossians 2:3). We need to tap into them and solve the problems our communities are facing. Believers need to identify with Jesus as the Creator by designing new software or coming up with a way to heal cancer. There are a great many challenges in today's world. The church must rise to the occasion and come up with the answers. Let us tap into some of that wisdom and knowledge that are hid in Christ our Lord to find the solutions.

God has a few favorite words and phrases that are close to His heart. Kingdom and business are two of them. There are different ways a kingdom advances. One of the major ways it does is through businesses. Another way is through military invasion. Military invasion causes conflicts and bloodshed. Business is the peaceful method of kingdom advancement.

Jesus shared a parable about the kingdom of heaven and how it advances in Matthew 13:33. "Another parable He spoke to them: 'The kingdom of heaven is like leaven, which a woman took and hid in three measures of meal till it was all leavened.'"

If I were to reword this in business terms, it would sound something like this: The kingdom of heaven is like a product a person invented; and through mass-producing and marketing, it filled the entire earth. As a result, the whole world benefitted from it."

When we think of business, most people think of an entity that makes money. But business is not limited to just making money. Business is a system of operation that, when applied, will produce an intended result or product. When God decided to expand His kingdom to earth, He established a business called the garden of Eden.

Eden was the biggest business enterprise anyone ever began in history. But it failed temporarily because the first manager God appointed to take care of that business failed to accomplish his assigned mission. Ever since, God has been trying to restore that business and its managers. God created us to manage this enormous planet and its vast resources for Him.

Every business and management principle ever used is mentioned in the first three chapters of Genesis. Whenever God decides to do something new, He introduces a new business. Kingdom business is the solution to alleviate poverty and hunger; with proper management, there would be no need of anyone being poor or living in hunger in the earth.

There is a company in Israel that purifies salt water from the ocean and makes it clean drinking water. It's one of the fastest growing companies in the world. Everyone needs water to survive. Most Islamic nations in the Middle East are deserts and do not have good drinking water, but they are close to oceans. What an opportunity for kingdom evangelism! You go in there to solve that problem, and put roots in the ground. America had the same opportunity in the Middle East when they discovered oil there many years ago. But again, they did not utilize that opportunity for kingdom purposes, only for monetary gain. How sad.

Today in India, the government is looking for companies from around the world to clean up the Ganges River. It's one of the dirtiest and most polluted rivers on earth, but it's also the most holy river for the Hindus. I personally know a brother who has such a company that came to meet with the government officials to talk about it. He is a Spirit-filled believer. They are negotiating the deal as I write this book.

Three Ways a Kingdom Advances

Military

In the ages past and even today, countries expand and invade other countries using their military. This causes much damage, bloodshed, and deep-rooted wounds between nations. In the spirit, evangelism is an invasion of God's army into enemy territory. Sometimes this causes problems and retaliation from the enemy.

Business

One modern-day example of kingdom advancement is the expansion of the British Empire. They used business tactics to expand their rule around the world; their military came later. They used trade to gain a footing in different nations and eventually took over the rule of those nations completely.

There is a difference between businesses that make money and kingdom businesses. I thought all businesses that made money and supported evangelism were kingdom businesses. The Holy Spirit said they are not. If a business supports winning souls to Christ, they are not helping God's kingdom on earth. They are only saving people to go to heaven, because in most parts of the world the gospel people preach is the religious, or the salvation, gospel.

There is a big difference between kingdom businesses and regular businesses. A kingdom business is a business that is committed to advancing God's kingdom on earth: to see His will be done on earth as it is in heaven. That is the reason they are established and exist. There are Christian businesses that support ministries greatly, but they are not necessarily kingdom businesses. There is a big difference between helping to do evangelism and seeing God's will done in a nation as it is in heaven, though a kingdom business will support world missions and evangelism as well.

A kingdom business is a business that helps solve a nation's problems. Kingdom business and Kingdom evangelism are connected because one of the ways you do kingdom evangelism is through kingdom business. That is the next point.

Solving Problems

One of the best ways to evangelize a nation or community is by solving its problems. When you solve a problem you, receive the support and respect of the people; and they will accept your message.

Kingdom Media

Through the media, we can see what the devil (the god of this world) is doing. Unfortunately, even Christians allow this garbage to freely flow into their homes. Through the media they fill themselves with junk and then come to church on Sunday and fall asleep when the Word is being preached. They try to live for God while their minds are filled with the trash of this world. They will never be successful this way.

A person is only as good as his mind, just like a computer is only as good as its processor and software. Most Christians know more about what is going on in the world than what is in the Bible. Others know more about their football team and its players than the names of the books and characters in the Bible.

The average American watches twenty hours of TV per week. Do you know how much time the average American spends reading the Bible or praying in a week? Fifteen minutes at the most. Do you know how much time the average pastor in America spends with the Lord in a week? Twenty-five minutes. Many preach ready-made sermons they buy from other ministries or resources. You try to send these Christians to win the world for Christ and they will get whipped by the enemy and come back home crying like a puppy. God, have mercy on us! We need to fill our minds and hearts with God's Word and spend time in Jesus' presence, if we are ever going to be able to stand against the evil we live in.

We need to use every form of media that is available to propagate the gospel of the kingdom. We need to take them back from the enemy and take dominion over it ourselves. Media has more influence on this present generation than anything else.

Kingdom Agriculture

The World's Agriculture Causes Diseases

When we preach the gospel of the kingdom it affects every aspect of our society. It brings total transformation. Keep that truth in mind as you read this section.

Chapter 7 | Administering the Kingdom of God, Part 3

Food-related sicknesses[65] are in the top ten causes of death in the world today. 11.3% of the world's population is hungry every day.[66] More than twenty thousand people die every single day because of hunger and hunger-related issues. Cancer is another major cause of premature death in the world today. 1,685,210 people will receive the bad news, "You have cancer" this year.[67] 8.2 million people die of cancer worldwide every year, and in the U.S. alone, 1,500 people die of cancer *every day*.[68] Every *year*, about 564,800 people in the US will die of cancer.[69] That is a staggering number. One morning a few months ago, as I was minding my own business, I heard a voice in my heart say, "I want to give you the key to cure cancer." I was as surprised as you are as you read this. But it was loud and clear. The reason I hesitated to believe this was because I do not have any training in medicine. Then I heard the rest, "Kingdom agriculture is the key to cure cancer." I kept that in my heart for a long time; I did not share it with anyone because I did not know how to explain it. I literally had no idea what I was talking about.

Many of the diseases that affect people today stem from our food. The root cause of every problem we see on this earth today began in Genesis because the first man and woman ate the forbidden fruit. So you can imagine the power of eating the wrong food. We are not supposed to eat what the world is producing. We have no idea how much poison we put into our bodies on a daily basis in the food and drinks we consume. The church is supposed to produce its own food. We are supposed to be better

---

65 "The top 10 causes of death," World Health Organization, January 2017, accessed February 16, 2017, http://www.who.int/mediacentre/factsheets/fs310/en/.

66 Food and Agricultural Organization of the UN, "The State of Food Insecurity in the World 2014," FAO, 2014, May 1, 2015, accessed February 16, 2017, https://www.dosomething.org/facts/11-facts-about-world-hunger.

67 "Cancer Statistics," National Cancer Institute, accessed February 16, 2017, https://www.cancer.gov/about-cancer/understanding/statistics.

68 Ibid.

69 "Helping Families Face the Challenges of Cancer," Cancer Facts, accessed February 10, 2017, http://www.thomlatimercares.org/Cancer_Facts.htm.

in health, finances, education, and family life than the rest of the world. We are God's children. The world should envy us, not the other way around.

I assume we all know at least one person whose life ended prematurely because of cancer. I don't believe that is God's will or plan. I don't have all the facts and proofs to tell you that kingdom agriculture will cure or eradicate cancer. This is yet to be proven. But I am happy to tell you that there are believers and Christian organizations in many parts of the world, including the US, which have already begun producing their own food. We have started such a project in India. I also have an invitation to visit two such ministries in South Africa and Malawi. I am believing that God will allow me to visit them, not only to encourage them, but also to learn from them. We are supposed to be the most productive people on earth. I encourage you to pray and ask God if you have any role to play in this.

The Dangers of Chemically and Genetically Altered Foods

Slowly, more revelation began to come to my spirit. One of the major causes of cancer is the food we eat and products we use at home. It is hard to find food these days that is not contaminated by some poison or altered by science. Hormones are injected into chickens and other animals to cause them to grow at a rate of speed that their body is not designed to handle. Naturally, a chicken takes close to six months to fully develop. The demand for chicken is so great there is no way farms can wait that long for a chick to develop, so they inject them with growth hormones and that same chicken matures in less than fifty days. These unnaturally produced chickens are what most people eat in restaurants and buy from stores.

When you eat such meat, that same hormone goes into your body. When a child eats chicken that has been injected with growth hormones, that child also begins to grow and mature at a faster rate than nature intended. In many cultures, some girls reach maturity before the age of ten. Scientists do not know what other effects the use of these hormones will have on our children.

When an adult eats such meat, it's a different story. An adult has already reached their maturity and growth level based on their age. When they eat hormone-injected meats, those hormones impact them negatively. Their cells begin to grow and multiply out of control and can end up developing cancer.

Genetically-modified grains, vegetables, and fruit are other altered forms of food we eat. To cause increased amounts of production and size, scientists have modified the genetic codes of these foods. The genetic code is written by the Creator. God knows how to make substances from which our bodies can gain nourishment. When you manipulate that to benefit financially, you are messing with God's order and laws and the result will not be good.

Another cause of food-related diseases is consuming meat, milk, and other products from mixed breeds. We are not supposed to mix breeds. God created each species according to its own kind. There is a specific command in the Bible not to do this.

> "You shall keep My statutes. You shall not let your livestock breed with another kind. You shall not sow your field with mixed seed. Nor shall a garment of mixed linen and wool come upon you" (Leviticus 19:19).

Chemicals and pesticides are applied to protect vegetables and fruit and anything that grows in the ground. They are very dangerous to the human body and mind, and cause malfunctions in our internal organs. We use various kinds of products and cleaning supplies that contain chemicals that are harmful to us too. Most of the time we are not even aware that these products are dangerous because they are so familiar to us.

Research or Prevention?

In the U.S. alone, six billion dollars are raised each year for breast cancer research and awareness.[70] For children's and other types of cancer, the

---

70 Lea Goldman, "The Big Business of Breast Cancer," Marie Claire, September 14, 2011, accessed February 16, 2017, http://www.marieclaire.com/politics/news/a6506/breast-cancer-business-scams/.

amount goes even higher. How these funds are being used is questionable. The number of people who are affected is growing every year. What if we spent a fraction of that amount for cancer prevention? We should be investing in organic farming and kingdom agriculture so the future generation will be totally free from the grip of cancer. As the age-old saying goes, "an ounce of prevention is worth a pound of cure." I am convinced it is possible to do this. The church needs to step up and step out of their comfort zone and come up with the solutions to the problems humanity is facing.

A great deal of research has taken place for cancer, yet no one has come up with the cure or effective ways to prevent it. Instead it has become a growing industry that generates billions of dollars each year, one of the fastest growing industries in the world. In 2014, global spending on cancer medications was $100 billion dollars.[71]

If we spent a fraction of that amount to prevent cancer, we can make this world cancer free in just ten years' time. As you know, the most effective way to prevent something is to find the cause of it and deal with it. Incredible amounts of money are being spent that is dealing with the "fruit" instead of the "root." As a kingdom citizen, my intention is to lay the axe to the root. I want every kingdom-minded believer to join me in this movement. Together, we can make a difference for Jesus and His kingdom and reveal to the world the greatness of our God.

I am focusing on cancer here, but there are scores of other diseases and sicknesses that are rooted in the food and products we consume. People have all kinds of health complications that were not common even fifty years ago. Allergies and reactions that were never heard of before are now occurring.

---

71 Kimberly Leonard, "Global Cancer Spending Reaches $100B," Usnews.com, May 5, 2015, accessed February 16, 2017, http://www.usnews.com/news/blogs/data-mine/2015/05/05/global-cancer-spending-reaches-100b.

What is the solution? Kingdom agriculture and the businesses and manufacturing that will spring from it is the solution. This means we must produce food and other products naturally in the most natural environments, which are uncontaminated by chemicals, growth hormones, pesticides, and genetic manipulation. Some call it organic food, but even so-called organic foods can be contaminated to a degree. Anything that comes packaged is not good for you.

It All Started with a Garden

We have to redeem the land before we start cultivating it, asking the Lord and the land to forgive us for the transgressions that were done on it. We should dedicate it to our Lord God who is the original Owner of the land. We ask the Lord to look upon the land, to care for it, and protect it. We ask God to be a partner in producing food because He is the One who created every living thing.

We bring the land into full alignment and harmony with heaven, based on Ephesians 1:10 and Colossians 1:20 because in Christ Jesus God reconciled all things that are in heaven and the things on earth. We need to appropriate this as any other spiritual truth.

God introduced His kingdom to the earth, not through a palace or concrete jungle, but through a garden. Why did He do that? Because He knows that human beings cannot live without food and that we become what we eat. That was the protocol. That was where God chose to begin to exercise His dominion on earth. There are two major reasons people die today. In one part of the world people are dying of hunger because there is a lack of food, and on the other side of the earth they are dying *because* of the food, through sicknesses and diseases that are rooted in eating food that is contaminated with various chemicals.

God did not give Adam a skyscraper, but a garden and agriculture, one of the foundations of kingdom economy. There are many countries where Christians are starving. That is totally unacceptable. They are born-again and Spirit-filled, but never heard the gospel of the kingdom. Jesus said when we seek His kingdom first in our lives, He would provide for our basic needs.

On the other side, many Christians are sick in their bodies because they are eating the wrong kind of food. That is unacceptable as well. We are supposed to be part of the solution and not the problem.

It's not unusual today to hear about babies born with all kinds of abnormalities and health issues. Most of these attacks stem from the food, medicine, or the environment to which the mother was exposed while pregnant. I keep hearing about children and young people who are diagnosed with terminal illnesses. These cases can be prevented if we apply the wisdom of God to our day-to-day living.

We have been running with only one side of the kingdom: healing, prophecy, crusades, and so on, but nations are not being transformed or impacted. There is another side to the kingdom, the natural side: government, economy, education, agriculture, and all the rest outlined here. Only when the kingdom of God begins to impact each of those components of a nation, will change come.

It Comes through a Tree

When God created Adam and put him in the garden, He said, "Of all the trees of the garden you may freely eat."[72]

God intended that our health and wellbeing would come from trees and plants. It is interesting to note that the cross is a tree. Salvation and healing for the whole world came through a tree.

It is also true that sickness and curse and death came through eating the fruit of a wrong tree: The Tree of the Knowledge of Good and Evil.

---

72 See Genesis 2:16.

The tree of life that we find both in the garden of Eden and in Revelation has leaves and fruit, which are for the healing of the nations. We can eat from the tree of life through Jesus Christ.[73] He is the bread of life.

When the Israelites were in the wilderness, they reached a place called Marah, where the water was not good to drink because it was bitter. The people complained to Moses and Moses cried out to God. God showed him a tree and when he put it into the water, the water turned sweet. The Lord revealed something about Himself that He had never revealed before through this: He is the Lord who heals us.

While in the wilderness, God fed the Israelites with food from heaven that kept them healthy and in an un-aging mode for forty years. That's the real power of eating the right kind of food!

Sickness and death came—and still comes—through eating the wrong food, just like healing and well-being come through eating the right food.

"The Lord will not allow the righteous soul to famish. But
He casts away the desires of the wicked" (Proverbs 10:3).

There are many people in this world who live in hunger. If God cares about people more than other creatures, why do so many people die for the lack of food? We just read that, "The Lord will not allow the righteous soul to famish." Who are the righteous and the wicked in God's sight? From a human view point there are people who look righteous and do good things with their lives, but they may not be righteous before God. Those who are righteous before God are those who trust in Jesus. We must trust in the provision He gave through His Son Jesus for our righteousness.

---

73 See Revelation 2:7 and 22:2, 14.

Chapter 8

Kingdom Evangelism, Part 1

"But you shall receive power when the Holy Spirit has come upon you; and you shall be witnesses to Me in Jerusalem, and in all Judea, and Samaria, and to the end of the earth" (Acts 1:8).

If you study the book of Acts in depth, you will find the secrets to bringing nations back to God. There is a specific method God used throughout Acts, which we can use to win any nation to Jesus Christ in a matter of time if we learn it and put it to work.

The apostles did not go out and conduct crusades and start orphanages or build old-age homes. They won nations to Christ. How did they do that? It is worth repeating that twelve men reached the entire known world in their lifetime, something more than a billion Christians have been trying to do for almost two thousand years.

What method did the Holy Spirit use? The church in the book of Acts functioned as any kingdom would operate. Only when we have the perception of a kingdom will we truly understand the book of Acts. Without a kingdom mindset we will only see the religious activities and miracles.

When a kingdom tries to take over another kingdom, it goes after people in key positions. In our case, we are not trying to kill them, but get them saved. After the Holy Spirit came, certain things were set in place in the early church before the miracles began to manifest. In Acts 2 the economy was set in order. Doctrines of the apostles were set in order. We do not pay attention to those; we jump straight to the miracle that happened in Acts 3.

New Methods of Kingdom Evangelism

We are used to personal evangelism, prayer evangelism, power evangelism, and crusade evangelism, but may not be familiar with kingdom evangelism. Though we have been doing other kinds of evangelism, nations are not being won to Christ. All other types of evangelism will bring some souls to heaven because they are all based on the religious gospel people have been preaching, but that is not the most efficient way to win souls.

Personally, I like them all. But if we add kingdom evangelism to them, we will have the missing ingredient and we will see the result we have been looking for, which is to win the nations for Christ. All other types of evangelism needs to come under the umbrella of kingdom evangelism, without which we will never see nations coming to Christ. The plan God gave me will enable the church to reach any country on this earth within ten to fifteen years, without a single crusade or healing rally! But it will take some serious praying, strategizing, planning, and re-training to accomplish that goal. The good news is you can see your nation come to Christ in your lifetime. That is exciting. I know that's the dream and prayer of every true believer of Jesus Christ. You may ask why ten to fifteen years? It will take that many years to train a generation to influence a culture.

When God decided to solve the problem man and earth had, He sent a King and a kingdom. He did not send a program or a new method. He knew the earth's problems would be solved only through an invasion of another kingdom.

If you are a child of God, you are part of His kingdom. Our ultimate goal through evangelism is to win nations to Christ. Kingdom evangelism invades the kingdom of darkness with the kingdom of God and infiltrates worldly systems with the ways of God.

If we are to win nations to Christ (which is God's heart), we need to preach the gospel of the kingdom and do kingdom evangelism. What is kingdom evangelism? *Kingdom evangelism is evangelizing through solving nations' and communities' problems, and witnessing to nations Jesus as King, Creator, Judge, and Lord.*

Kingdom evangelism is done through three major avenues. One is solving nations' and communities' problems. Second, witnessing to key leaders of nations, communities, and businesses, or influencing them with the wisdom of God. Third, witnessing Jesus as King, Creator, Judge, and Lord. To do this, kingdom citizens must occupy, or influence, key places of leadership in politics, business, media, education, land, and other areas of life.

Evangelism through Problem Solving

How is kingdom evangelism accomplished? First of all, through problem solving. We read in Genesis about the famine the nation of Egypt faced. Actually, it was a famine that was caused by God.

> "Moreover He called for a famine in the land; He destroyed all the provision of bread" (Psalm 105:16).

God will cause problems to arise in nations, giving an opportunity for God's people to step in and solve them. But in most cases, when such problems arise, Christians miss the opportunity and start complaining and crying, "Lord, have mercy, take us out of here." It's either that or they point to the problems as signs of the end times. In any of these scenarios they do nothing, much to their loss.

In Egypt, the problem was a famine and God gave Joseph the wisdom to solve the problem. Thankfully, he did not blame global warming for the famine. He presented the plan to the king, who accepted the plan and gave the order to execute it. Within fourteen years, the entire nation of Egypt was evangelized. They knew there was a God in heaven that ruled over the nations. As a result, both Joseph and Pharaoh became extremely wealthy because toward the end of the famine people began to sell their land and property to Joseph for food. We can apply the same principle and reach any nation with the gospel of the kingdom within ten to fifteen years of time.

To introduce the Kingdom of God to this earth, God used a Garden (Agriculture). To reach the nation of Egypt God struck it's agriculture sector with a famine. Through Joseph He introduced Kingdom Agriculture to solve that problem. He can use one or more aspects of His kingdom to reach a nation. He is looking for kingdom-minded people through whom He can introduce His wisdom to solve problems nations are facing.

Every nation on this earth is ripe for harvest: They are facing tremendous problems in every sector of life. We have been interpreting this as the signs of the end times. But those signs have been there from the beginning of time. Famine was there in Egypt, and famine is happening now in different nations. There was even a famine mentioned in the book of Acts.[74] Wars have always been there, and wars are here now in many parts of the world.

You may say that to solve these problems will cost billions of dollars and you do not have the money. It may or may not cost any money to solve national problems. How much money did it take for Joseph to save Egypt from such a severe famine? Not a penny!

How can a person, without using any money, solve the biggest problem a nation faces? I will share with you a secret, and this will work in

---

74 See Acts 11:28.

any nation. There is something more precious than money and gold. It is more powerful than weapons of war.[75] That is the wisdom of God, and that is what manifested through Joseph. You may say that you do not have any wisdom either. The Bible says if we lack wisdom to ask God who gives it liberally.[76]

Communities around us have problems that only God's wisdom can solve. Those problems are waiting for us to get out of the four walls, which we call church, and solve them to show that our God is greater and wiser and smarter than the gods of any nation. I am not talking about handing out free food. We are good at that.

Many nations are struggling to feed their citizens. There are many communities who do not have access to clean drinking water. Many don't have schools, and other basic necessities of life. Horrific abuse of women and children is going on in many countries. People are depressed and hopeless. They do not know their purpose. They are all waiting for the gospel of the kingdom to be preached to them.

Evangelism through Influencing Key Leaders

In Acts we read about Philip the Evangelist, who was led by the Holy Spirit to the wilderness of Gaza to witness to one of the leaders of the nation of Ethiopia. The eunuch, who was in charge of the treasury (economy) of the Queen of Ethiopia, was traveling back to his nation after visiting Jerusalem for the feast.

Philip witnessed to him about Jesus, and this eunuch gave his life to the Lord and was baptized. I believe he returned to his country and became a witness for Jesus Christ. He was a man of influence.

---

75 See Ecclesiastes 9:16,18.

76 See James 1:5.

Consider the people Paul won to the kingdom. Many were influential. They were leaders, either religious, community, business, or political.

Evangelism through Witnessing Jesus as King, Judge, and Lord

There are more people who are called to be in government and positions of authority than any other type of calling in the church. In Scripture, God used these people to influence kings and direct kingdoms. We have many more people in the body of Christ today with the same calling, but they have never been taught or trained in their calling so they sit in our pews, frustrated and angry about what is happening in their nations and governments. These people need to be trained and released to become prime ministers, presidents, and community leaders.

I would like to say a few words about witnessing Jesus as Lord. Lord means owner. We have landlords and other people we call lord in some cultures. To witness Jesus as Lord, Christians need to own land and properties. The first thing we should do when we move into a new community is buy a piece of land. You may say that you don't have money to do so. Believe the Lord for the money because He owns it all; the devil is illegally occupying that land until someone who has legal and spiritual authority comes in and dispossesses him.

Jesus is not just our Lord. He is the Lord of this earth. He is the Lord of heaven and earth.

> "The earth *is* the Lord's, and all its fullness, the world and those who dwell therein" (Psalm 24:1).

Jesus said, "Go into all the world and preach the gospel to all creation." Why does all creation need the gospel and not just humans? The curse affected everything. Paul said that he preached the gospel to every creature under heaven. Why does every creature need to hear the gospel? Because they all came under bondage after the fall of man. Salvation is not just for humans, but also for every aspect of creation that was affected by the fall of man. You are anointed to set free a part of creation from its bondage.

> "If indeed you continue in the faith, grounded and steadfast, and are not moved away from the hope of the gospel which you heard, which was preached to every creature under heaven, of which I, Paul, became a minister" (Colossians 1:23).

There are over seven billion people on earth today and only two billion are thought to be Christians. That means more than five billion people are yet to be reached. But we have more Christians, miracle workers, technology, and resources today than at any other time before. Is there a solution? I believe there is. The solution is administering the kingdom of God. The question is how do we do that?

If we use the methods we currently use, based on the results we are seeing, it may take another two thousand years to reach another billion souls. Within that time period, close to a hundred generations will live and die without ever knowing Jesus Christ. Is there a better and speedier way to reach more people? I strongly believe there is, and I am excited to share that with you. That is what I wish to explore in the next two chapters.

We Can Reach Our World

This is not something new I invented. It's been in the Bible all along from the very beginning. It is God's way of reaching the world. It is called "kingdom evangelism." The apostles used the same method and before they died, the majority of the world was Christian. There is only one agency God put on this earth to evangelize the world and that is the church. But the church, as a whole, has lost its mission and is running parallel to the world system.

Why kingdom evangelism? The early church and the apostles lived and ministered in a very hostile society. People like Moses, Joseph, Nehemiah,

Daniel, and Esther were all living in environments that were hostile to their faith too. And today we find ourselves in a similar situation: living in a world in which it seems people are becoming more anti-Christian and anti-gospel. But those who lived before all reached their world for God. The question is how did they do it? They did it through kingdom evangelism.

We need to address evangelism with a kingdom mindset, a mindset of one who is part of a kingdom that is trying to take over another kingdom. What approach would they take? Did they go to the enemy's kingdom and sing songs? Or did they reach the poor and preach on their streets? I believe the answer is no. We must make a plan to *influence* each of the components that the kingdom is made of, or the people who are in authority, those governing the kingdom. In this case, the kingdom of God is taking over the kingdom of darkness.

Kingdom Evangelism requires kingdom warfare. You might be familiar with the term spiritual warfare. We need to identify the source of the warfare to effectively tackle it. It is coming from a kingdom. If two kingdoms are going to battle for a region, in our case they are, how do they prepare the battle strategy? What are the places they would consider a stronghold?

If you look at the world today, the majority do not make the decisions for the general public. It's not the majority that influence and shape a culture, but the few people or that one person at the top that makes decisions for everybody. So if you want to reach a nation, you try to reach those people or train Christians to be in those positions. That is how kingdom evangelism works.

In any arena: business, politics, or entertainment, it's the top three percent of the population that make decisions for the rest of us. They shape the culture of every nation. The rest just follow their lead. Unless we have influence with that three percent, we are not going to see any change for the better in our nations in the near future. You can scream and shout all you want inside the four walls of a building or even on the street, but nothing is going to change unless we learn to think and act like our God. That is what we are supposed to be doing anyway. We are His children after all.

Wherever I go people tell me how prosperous the Jewish people are. They always come up among that three percent in different arenas of life, regardless of which nation they are in. How do they do that? The common response is "They are God's chosen and blessed people. Are born again Christians not chosen and blessed as well?" The difference is in the mindset. They have a kingdom mindset. You do not see Jewish people conducting crusades and worship nights in cities and in their synagogues. They are busy studying the laws that govern a nation and carving out a plan of how to influence it.

Most Christians think and act like second class citizens with a poverty mindset, without understanding what it means that God made us sit together with Christ in the heavenly places. We are partakers of the same promise and blessings that God gave to the Jewish people in the Old Testament and more. To be honest, we have received a better covenant than they. It's time to believe and act like it.

I am not saying we should have Christian presidents legislate the law for everyone to go to church. No. What I am saying is that if we have a Christian president or have a judiciary that believes the Bible, at least they will not legalize same-sex marriage or abortion. We can decide what our children are being taught in our schools and we can regulate what can be put on public television.

The Early Church

After the church was born, it reached people in every level of society. People from all walks of life were members of the church: the priests, rulers, government officials, widows, business people, and so on.

When the church was birthed on Pentecost, there were leaders and business people from every nation under heaven present in Jerusalem.

"And there were dwelling in Jerusalem Jews, devout men, *from every nation under heaven*" (Acts 2:5). The gospel was preached to every nation as a witness. There were devout and prominent men there from every nation.

When we think about Pentecost, we often limit it to an emotional experience. What was God thinking when He sent the Holy Spirit on that day? He had a kingdom mindset. He was thinking about how to influence key people from every nation in one setting. Bang! Mission accomplished. I call that a maximum impact!

Of course it was an emotional experience. When the Holy Spirit came, people thought the disciples were drunk. But what was the objective God was trying to accomplish through all this? Some people like to get emotional, crawl on the floor, and be called Holy Rollers, but that experience does not reach people of influence for the kingdom. We have been trying to duplicate the upper room experience but are not producing the same results they had. It is time for a change. God may have an entirely different strategy to reach the people of our time.

Do you remember the story of Philip the evangelist? An angel of the Lord told him to go by the road from Jerusalem to Gaza. He wanted Philip to meet a very influential man from the government of Ethiopia.

> "Now an angel of the Lord spoke to Philip, saying, 'Arise and go toward the south along the road which goes down from Jerusalem to Gaza.' This is desert. So he arose and went. And behold, a man of Ethiopia, a eunuch of great authority under Candace the queen of the Ethiopians, who had charge of all her treasury, and had come to Jerusalem to worship" (Acts 8:26-27).

This chief financial officer for the queen of Ethiopia is one example of the type of person who used to come to Jerusalem to worship. These are the kinds of people who were present at Pentecost. God took maximum advantage of this opportunity.

When the Gentiles were first reached with the gospel, God sent Peter to a particular man named Cornelius and his family. Cornelius was a centurion of the Roman army, a key person to reaching the Gentiles. A centurion is a commander over groups of a hundred soldiers, a man of influence among all the Jews and Gentiles (Acts 10:22). Why did God send Peter to Cornelius? Why not just ask him to start an outreach to orphans? No, God is a king and whatever He does has a kingdom flavor. I am not saying we should not take care of orphans and widows; we should, but to reach a nation or community we need to start from the top. Another example is the conversation Jesus had with Nicodemus. Nicodemus was a ruler of the Jews (John 3:1).

The Greatest Impact

Jesus was sent at the perfect time to have the greatest effect. The Bible says,

> "When the fullness of the time had come, God sent forth His Son" (Galatians 4:4).

What does it mean by the fullness of the time? Why did it take more than four thousand years for God to send His Son? God waited for the geopolitical setup of the world to be just right to reach more people with the good news of the gospel.

When Jesus was born, the Romans were in charge. The Romans were tolerant of some things and not at all of others. They took over territory and demanded tribute, allowing people to continue as they did before, as long as they did not threaten Roman authority or superiority. They ruled through an army that acted with order and precision, and they built good roads, which made traveling much easier than it had ever been before. They spoke one language, so that anyone who spoke Greek could easily share their message all over the vast Roman Empire.

Their empire was similar to America today. Everyone wanted what the Romans had: language, culture, food, lifestyle, citizenship, everything.

If one could have influence in Rome, he had influence everywhere. All over the world today people look to America and want what we have. If you want to reach the world, reach the most influential country, and all other countries will be reached automatically. That is what God meant when He said He sent Jesus at the fullness of the time, or the right time. He is so smart.

If we study the ministry of Paul and the churches he established, we will see that he was operating with a kingdom mindset. He did not go to a city to set up an orphanage or feeding program. God led him to people of influence. In Philippi, Paul and his team met a businesswoman named Lydia. The Lord opened her heart to hear the things spoken by Paul (Acts 16:14). The next convert was the jailor and his family because Paul and Silas were imprisoned as the result of casting a demon out of a girl, and God delivered them from the prison by sending an earthquake (Acts 16:16-33). Later in Thessalonica many prominent men and women believed the gospel and joined Paul and Silas and a new church was established.

> "And some of them were persuaded; and a great multitude of the devout Greeks, and not a few of the leading women, joined Paul and Silas" (Acts 17:4).

> "Therefore many of them believed, and also not a few of the Greeks, prominent women as well as men" (Acts 17:12).

> In Corinth we see the same pattern. The first converts in Corinth were a ruler of the synagogue named Crispus and his household (Acts 18:8).

When you reach people of influence, a domino effect takes place. In the eastern world, community is vibrant and plays an important role in a person's life. They don't think individualistically as in the western world. They adhere to the moral and social beliefs of their community leaders. They are watching and thinking about what other people are doing and are influenced by it.

The church reaches for the poor first because we have lost the kingdom mindset and no longer have a full revelation of who Jesus is. Because of this, we fail to witness effectively. Though many claim to have been preaching the full gospel, the truth is they have been preaching a partial gospel.

You Shall Receive Power

How do we practically implement kingdom evangelism into our daily lives? I have been in ministry a long time and have preached from Acts 1:8 many times; I thought I knew what it meant until the Holy Spirit began to show me a revelation contained in it that I never saw before. We have been limiting the Holy Spirit and His power to only use His gifts. Jesus did not say, "You shall receive gifts when the Holy Spirit comes upon you." If the power is only meant for gifts then Jesus would have said so. I was asking God why the church seemed so powerless in many cultures, even though the Christians were in the majority and they had received the power of the Holy Spirit.

The Holy Spirit began to open up the eyes of my understanding. Every believer who received the Holy Spirit has the power of God residing in him or her. But we have been using that power only for casting out demons, healing the sick, and prophesying over people.

There is a misconception in the church that if someone does not cast out demons, prophesy or heal the sick, they are not operating in the power of God. That is absolutely wrong. We cannot limit the power of the Holy Spirit. Those are just some gifts of the Holy Spirit. The Holy Spirit is much bigger than those gifts. He is the Architect of the entire universe.

The power of the Holy Spirit does not manifest the same way through every individual. He differs from person to person. We all use electricity; in the West we call electricity power. We use electricity for various purposes. We have scores of appliances and equipment in our homes that work with electricity. A refrigerator keeps things cold and a heater keeps us warm. A television allows us to see what's going on around the world. A computer helps to do various tasks. But the power that works behind all of these is electricity. It is the same power but with different manifestations.

Same Power—Different Manifestation

The same Holy Spirit that worked through Paul to cast out demons helped Joseph to administer a nation. The same Holy Spirit that helped Joseph to administer a nation helped David kill a giant. It was the same Power but different manifestations. Each believer in a church is like a different piece of equipment, or the Bible calls us vessels. We are unique and different and we each have a different function. So the power of God manifests through us differently. What if everyone was a healer? Then who would teach the adult classes and who would minister to the children? It's time to remove the limits we have put on the Holy Spirit.

> "There are diversities of gifts, but the same Spirit. There are differences of ministries, but the same Lord. And there are diversities of activities, but it is the same God who works all in all" (1 Corinthians 12:4-6).

> "If the whole body *were* an eye, where *would be* the hearing? If the whole *were* hearing, where *would be* the smelling? But now God has set the members, each one of them, in the body just as He pleased" (1 Corinthians 12:17-18).

In Deuteronomy 8 we read that it is God who gives us power to make wealth. Some people are anointed to create wealth. Some people are anointed to serve. Some people are anointed to minister to children. Some are anointed to be in politics. Again, it is the same power but different manifestations. There are some basic gifts that any believer can exercise: praying for the sick, giving a word to someone who is discouraged, taking authority over demons. But don't get stuck there or try to become a specialist. You might be called to do much more and possibly something different.

That means that if you have a product or mastered an ability, skill, or service, it is a witness of the gospel to unbelievers. If a believer is a CEO of a national or multinational corporation, his position and work ethic are a witness of the gospel to everyone around him, without doing any *preaching*. This is kingdom evangelism.

This revelation answered my long-unanswered question about why the church has been unable to reach the majority of the population of the earth. We have been trying to fly with one wing. In many parts of the world, especially in the West, I believe we have already reached the maximum people we can with the methods that we traditionally know and practice: crusades, revivals, healing rallies, gospel tracts, etc. If the rest of the world is to be reached, the church needs to take hold of this revelation and apply it.

New Age: New Methods

The leaders that God used in the last century for crusades, healings, and tent meetings are ready to pass their baton to the next generation. Some already have. But in every generation, God does something new. If we try to copy our previous generations we will totally miss what God has for us now. There is a new generation that God is raising up. They are not sure of their identity yet because they lack direction and training. Right now they are trying to copy what they have seen from their leaders, but that will not work for them.

Just look at the churches: most are no longer effective in what they are doing. They are in survival mode and ready to crumble. They are carrying out their traditions and doing fun things to keep people interested. Many know something different must happen but they lack direction so they try to repeat something that happened in the 60s or 80s.

Let me ask you a question. Would you like to go back to using anything you used in the 60s and 80s right now? Your style of clothing, the cars you drove, the electronics and technology you used, or the food you ate? Do you think our children want to do that? No, they wouldn't. Then why do you think the *spiritual* things that worked then would work now? They will not. What God did then was for that generation.

Now is the time for kingdom evangelism. It is evangelism that occurs as a by-product or as a result of the body of Christ worldwide administering the kingdom of God in their communities and nations. This is not a new kind of evangelism. It's a restoration of the true method mentioned all throughout the Bible, a method the church is neglecting because of ignorance and deception.

People like Abraham, Joseph, Daniel, Esther, Nehemiah, and many others never preached a sermon or healed the sick, but they lived their life with a kingdom mindset and executed God's purposes through their lives in nations and over kingdoms. As a result of this process, *kingdom evangelism* took place, meaning nations and kings came to know that there is a God in heaven that ruled over them.

The people who are not yet reached may not come to a crusade or healing rally. We need to employ a different method. "Behold, I will do a new thing, now it shall spring forth; shall you not know it?" (Isaiah 43:19). As you receive this revelation and move according to it, you will be that person God is waiting to use to change the world with the kingdom of God.

God gave each of us the power of the Holy Spirit to become a witness for Jesus. He said to me, "Before you go out and witness for Jesus, you need to know who Jesus is." I thought I knew who Jesus was because of my background. I had been brought up in a Christian home and had been in church all my life. But when the Holy Spirit began to reveal to me who Jesus is, I understood why the church is not effective in many cultures. It is because we have not only limited the Holy Spirit but also limited Jesus in what we know of Him and how we have been witnessing Him to the world. We have reached the world we could with the knowledge we have of who Jesus is. If the rest of the world is going to be reached, we need to know what we do not know of Jesus and witness for Him accordingly. Then the rest will be history. So let's find out who Jesus really is and learn how to witness for Him.

1) Creator

First, the Holy Spirit said Jesus is the Creator of the universe. Everything you see with your eyes (and even what you cannot see) was created by Jesus. How do we witness Jesus as the Creator?

> *"All things were made through Him,* and without Him nothing was made that was made" (John 1:3).

> *"For by Him all things were created* that are in heaven and that are on earth, visible and invisible" (Colossians 1:16).

> "And to make all see what is the fellowship of the mystery, which from the beginning of the ages has been hidden in God who created all things through Jesus Christ" (Ephesians 3:9).

People with products have influence. Governments of this world for the most part are influenced or controlled by people in business. How do we witness that Jesus is the Creator? The church needs to come up with products that are useful for the people in the world. The majority of our money is spent on products and services. Every day everyone uses products. Every product we use comes out of the earth.

God did not create airplanes, but He created the raw materials necessary to make them and hid them in the earth. God did not create furniture, but He created trees and gave us a brain to imagine and create what we needed from them. God did not create automobiles, but He created everything we needed to make one. Now it's up to us to use our imagination to make what we need. God gave us the earth, but we have not used it the best we can. Unfortunately, we have been waiting to get out of our planet. What a sad dilemma!

In most countries, key companies have more influence than the worldwide church combined. What if some of those companies were run by believers? It is time for the church to reclaim lost territories and to emerge as innovators like our Lord Jesus Christ. The Holy Spirit is the Architect of the Universe in which we exist, and the earth is just one tiny planet in that universe. I once read that the Sun can contain one million earth-sized planets. It is time to take the Holy Spirit out of the box we put Him in. We thought He came just to heal the sick, help us speak in tongues, and give us emotional experiences.

Many people turn their brain off when they are born again. We need to use our brains to come up with products and services that are helpful to humanity and become valuable to our society—not a nuisance! We need to open our minds and become productive and creative.

All the treasures of wisdom and knowledge are hid in Christ (Colossians 2:3). We need to tap into them and solve the problems our communities are facing. Believers need to identify with Jesus as the Creator by designing new software or coming up with a way to heal cancer. There are a great many challenges in today's world. The church must rise to the occasion and come up with the answers. Let us tap into some of that wisdom and knowledge that are hid in Christ our Lord to find the solutions.

2) King

Our God is a King.

> "The Lord *is King* forever and ever" (Psalm 10:16a).

> "For the *king*dom *is* the Lord's, and He rules over the nations" (Psalm 22:28).

> He is also called the King of glory (Psalm 24:8).

> "Where is He who has been born King of the Jews? For we have seen His star in the East and have come to worship Him" (Matthew 2:2).

> "Now to the King eternal, immortal, invisible, to God who alone is wise, *be* honor and glory forever and ever. Amen" (1 Timothy 1:17).

Chapter 8 | Kingdom Evangelism, Part 1

There were many in the Old Testament who witnessed God as King on the earth. Why don't we see this in our day? Did God cease from being a king? Let us find that out.

"For unto us a Child is born, unto us a Son is given; and the government will be upon His shoulder. And His name will be called Wonderful, Counselor, Mighty God, Everlasting Father, Prince of Peace. Of the increase of *His* government and peace *there will be* no end, upon the throne of David and over His kingdom, to order it and establish it with judgment and justice from that time forward, even forever. The zeal of the Lord of hosts will perform this" (Isaiah 9:6-7).

The above verses are prophetic declarations about our Lord Jesus Christ. The first thing it says about Him is that the government will be upon His shoulder. How does government rest upon His shoulders? He is the Head of the church and we are His body on this earth. The shoulder is part of the body, which means the government of this earth is supposed to be on the shoulders of the church. For some reason we made this verse part of our eschatology, meaning something that is going to take place somewhere out there in the future. This is not true according to the verse. That is what religion does. It steals from us what we should have now and gives us a false hope that someday things are going to be better. But faith says, "now."

From the phrase "from that time forward, even forever" we understand that the fulfillment of the prophetic timing began from the time a Son was given. It says that of the increase of His government and peace, there will be no end. That means it is eternal. We all know the Son spoken of here is Jesus. He came two thousand years ago to order His government with judgment and justice from that time forward, even forever. Literally, it began two thousand years ago, but we have not grasped what it really meant.

When the wise men from the East came to see Jesus they came looking for the King who was born in Bethlehem. How did they receive the revelation that Jesus was a king? Because of His star they saw in the East

(Matthew 2:2). When He died, He died as a king too. The inscription on the cross was "King of the Jews." When the governor asked Jesus if He was the King of the Jews, He did not deny it. He said, "It is as you say" (Matthew 27:11).

How do we witness to others of Jesus as a king? Believers need to be involved in the political arena of their nations. We have been avoiding politics for too long. Because of that, the unrighteous have taken over governments all over the world. There is no righteous justice system in the world anymore. People with money make their own rules. Any wicked person with money can do almost anything anywhere in the world.

Isaiah said the government shall be upon the shoulders of Jesus (Isaiah 9:6), not on the shoulders of the devil. Church leaders should encourage believers to get involved in politics, both locally and in the central government of their nations. Otherwise, how do we witness to others that Jesus is King?

One of the main reasons this world is in this chaos is because there are not very many people witnessing Jesus as a king. "When *the righteous are in authority,* the people rejoice: but when the wicked beareth rule, the people mourn" (Proverbs 29:2 KJV).

Anytime I meet someone from any country, they are always complaining about how bad the government in their nation is, and they talk against the leaders of their nations. Just talking negative about your government is not going to change anything for the better. The only way to change anything is if we have witnesses for Jesus in those governments. We need believers in positions of influence for the kingdom causes we are striving for. We must find out why we do not have any influence in government and come up with a solution.

One of the popular messages of the last few years was telling Americans to go back to her roots; that message is dying out as I write this book. America cannot go back to her roots. We need a new strategy.

Chapter 8 | Kingdom Evangelism, Part 1

There were fifty-six men who signed the Declaration of Independence. Out of the fifty-six, fifty-four of them were known to be Christians and attended some form of church. That meant their moral and ethical value system was based on Judeo-Christian ethics. That is why this country was established the way it was. How many people do we have in our government now that are a witness for Jesus? If we are going to take this country back to its roots, we need believers in positions of government—at both the state and national levels— who will witness Jesus as a king.

Again, we are not here to take over governments, but like Joseph and Daniel did, we need to have people witnessing in high places. Everyone God used in the Old Testament is a type of Christ: Moses, Joseph, David, Daniel, and Esther. Every single person God used manifested Christ through their life and His mission on earth. We have received the real deal, and today there are fewer witnesses for Jesus than ever in world governments.

God has anointed many people with His power to be a witness in government, but they have avoided it, thinking it is not God's will for them. The enemy has deceived us to keep us out of this most important aspect of a nation so that he can have free reign without any hindrance. Every government on earth belongs to Jesus, because there is no authority, natural or spiritual, except from Him. Why should we give the authority God gave us to the devil and then complain about what he is doing with it? Paul calls people in governmental authority "ministers." Did you know that? In Romans 13 he mentioned it two times. I was really surprised when I read this.

> "For he is the minister of God to thee for good" (Romans 13:4a KJV).

> "For this cause pay ye tribute also: for they are God's ministers, attending continually upon this very thing" (Romans 13:6 KJV).

I am a minister of the gospel. I preach the gospel to groups of people. You can be in charge of finance in the government of your nation and you are also a minister of God. You preach the gospel through your influence, your input, and your decisions. The same Holy Spirit is working through us, but in different manifestations.

There is a wrong teaching in the body of Christ that kings are those people who do business. That is not entirely true. Kings might do business, but their primary role is to be in government.

Each believer is anointed to manifest at least one aspect of Jesus. When we all come together as a body, we have the fullness of God (Ephesians 4:13). Church, this has to happen. It must happen if Jesus is going to return to the earth. He is not coming for a church crying like a baby to get her out of the earth. He is coming for a victorious church.

Every person God used in the Old Testament was a type or shadow of Christ, so that means they were representing or foreshadowing Christ who was to come. Abraham was a prophet, Joseph was a prime minister, and David was a king. Esther was a queen, Moses was a deliverer, and the list goes on. They were all witnesses of the Messiah. Jesus is all of them and more. Jesus said every Scripture testifies of Him.

> "You search the Scriptures, for in them you think you have eternal life; and these are they which *testify* of Me" (John 5:39).

3) Judge

> "The Lord executes righteousness and justice *for all* who are oppressed" (Psalm 103:6).

> "And He commanded us to preach to the people, and to testify that it is He who was ordained by God *to be* **Judge** of the living and the dead" (Acts 10:42).

If the Lord executes righteousness and justice for *all* who are oppressed, how does He accomplish it and why do we not see that happening in our world today? Does our God lie? There are millions of people who are oppressed and in need of justice. The only way God can do it is through His people, the *ekklesia*.

If there was ever a time we needed to witness Jesus as the righteous Judge, it is now. The justice systems of the world are corrupt and have no moral foundation. We need judges that represent the kingdom in every level of our judicial system. Money manipulates almost every part of the justice system in the world today. The person with money can get around any crime.

When Jesus shared a parable about persistent prayer He mentioned an unrighteous judge and a widow, and how this widow kept imploring him. He finally gave in and avenged her.

> "Then the Lord said, 'Hear what the unjust judge said. And shall God not avenge His own elect who cry out day and night to Him, though He bears long with them? I tell you that He will avenge them speedily. Nevertheless, when the Son of Man comes, will He really find faith on the earth?' " (Luke 18:6-8).

God is a judge and judges among the mighty.

> "God stands in the congregation of the mighty; He judges among the gods. How long will you judge unjustly, and show partiality to the wicked? *Selah*. Defend the poor and fatherless; do justice to the afflicted and needy. Deliver the poor and needy; free *them* from the hand of the wicked" (Psalm 82:1-4).

Who are those called mighty here? The Hebrew word used for mighty is *El,* the same word used for God in many places in the Bible. God calls us gods with a small "g."

The Supreme Court justices in the United States ruled to amend the definition of marriage. Christians across the country made an uproar in their churches and on social media but that did not change anything. If we need to change the rule, then we need Christians in the positions of lawmakers and judges. We need witnesses for Jesus as judges.

4) Prophet/Shepherd/Healer

The reason I put these three titles together is because we are very familiar with those ministry gifts. We have many prophets, pastors, and evangelists today that witness Jesus very effectively, so I am not going to spend much time on these areas. We are already familiar with Jesus as Prophet, and those who witness for Jesus that way we call prophets. Jesus is also Healer and those who witness for Him in this way we call healing evangelists.

5) Teacher

One of the names people called Jesus while He was on this earth was Teacher. How do we witness Jesus as the teacher? I believe the best schools and universities in any city or country should be under the leadership of Christians. That's the way we should witness Jesus as the teacher. Part of the Great Commission Jesus gave was: "Teaching them to observe all things that I have commanded you" (Matthew 28:20). Catholics have done a tremendous job in this area. In almost any country or city you visit, you will find a Catholic school with excellent standards. Even in Muslim countries, there are schools run by Catholics. Most of the leaders in their countries received their education in those schools. Why do the evangelicals not do such things? We need to sing and preach less and do more with our hands and brain and show the world that our God reigns. I believe God intended all forms of education to be done through the church.

6) Father

God called Abraham to be a father of many nations. Why a father? Why not an owner or a king? Nations need fathers. Fatherlessness is a key problem in our society today. Most people grow up without a good father and most do not receive the blessing of a good father. The second most important relationship we have is our relationship with our father. If our relationship with our father is not right, then nothing else will go right.

I cannot emphasize the importance of the blessing of a father. A person who is blessed by his or her father is an unstoppable force on this earth. Even the kingdom of darkness cannot do anything against that person because the blessing that was spoken will work as shield against all opposition. It is the same with cursing. A person who is cursed by his father has little hope. Serious repentance and healing must take place to break that curse. Otherwise, that curse will work like a 'lid" over his or her head; he or she will not go much higher in life.

I have noticed in many cultures that people die at an early age, especially men. When I visited some of these cultures I discovered that none of those people were ever blessed by their parents. The first commandment with a promise is to honor your father and mother so that it may go well with you and you will live long on the face of the earth. Your life span is directly connected to your relationship with your parents. How deep is that?

We need to witness Jesus as Father to the fatherless on this earth. It is not an easy task. I raised orphan children for fourteen years in our ministry and I know the challenges that are involved with it. In the place you were not blessed by your natural parents, God will connect you with a person who will be your spiritual father.

We must make sure we do not abuse or take advantage of those who are entrusted to us. We must not take spiritual fathering to an extreme either. We must make sure everything is balanced with the Word. God is a father to the fatherless (Psalm 68:5).

7) Redeemer

Jesus paid the price and redeemed our lives from death and destruction. There are many ways we can be a witness for Jesus as the Redeemer, but it might take a lot of sacrifice to witness to someone as their redeemer. One of the reasons for the many suicides, child labor, and prostitution in Third World countries is financial debt. People borrow money and are unable to pay it back or pay the interest, so they decide to end their life. Or, they are forced to send their children to work in factories or prostitution.

Most of the time it is not even very much money, less than a thousand dollars, but in many parts of the world that's a lot of money. I have had a few experiences where God helped me to witness as a redeemer in such cases. You won't believe the relief and freedom people feel and the joy you can see in their faces when their burden is lifted. Debt, in any sense, is a burden and a curse.

Slavery is still a problem today. Men, women, and children are sold as slaves in some parts of the world. We can witness Jesus as Redeemer if we pay their ransom and redeem them from slavery. I watched online how Christian women and children are being auctioned off in a Middle Eastern country. Because of persecution, many Christians from Pakistan fled to Thailand to seek asylum. When they arrived they were put in prison by the government for not paying the penalty. There are plenty of opportunities in the world to witness for Jesus as a redeemer.

8) Servant

Jesus said the Son of Man came to serve and give His life as a ransom for many (Matthew 20:28). When we serve we need to serve with a spirit of excellence. Whether you are working in a company or a hotel, in any capacity you serve other people, you serve as a witness for Jesus. You should not preach about Jesus; that's not what I mean by witnessing for Jesus. But by seeing the excellent work you do, people should ask you the reason behind your performance. Then you should say you are a witness of Jesus who also came to this earth to serve others.

Companies and institutions should stand in line to hire a Christian as their employee. They should be aware of the rare privilege it is to have a believer in Christ working for them. They should know about the increased level of excellence and quality we demonstrate in our work ethic. Church, what would happen in this world if the believers demonstrated the character and quality of Jesus in the workplace?

9) Giver/Rich

Jesus gave His life as a ransom for many (Mark 10:45). We know the famous verse, "God so loved the world He gave His only begotten Son." When you truly love someone you give everything. You give the most precious thing you have.

> "For you know the grace of our Lord Jesus Christ, that though He was rich, yet for your sakes He became poor, that you through His poverty might become rich" (2 Corinthians 8:9).

There is no reason for anyone to be poor on the earth, just as there is no reason for anyone to live in sin. Jesus became poor and paid for the poverty of the entire world. If anyone is living in sin or poverty, it is because of choice or ignorance. Most people are poor because of their ignorance. As kingdom citizens, we need to learn the laws that govern wealth and money and teach others how to create wealth. That's part of our mandate.

People have taken this truth to an extreme and developed a gospel called the prosperity gospel. There is no such gospel in the Bible. The gospel does bring blessings; there is no doubt about it, but we need to keep our focus on Jesus, not on our wealth or creating wealth.

Most of the prosperity preachers we have today do not preach or equip the believers to create wealth. They steal from the sheep and become rich. A true minister of the gospel is always looking for the betterment of the people he is teaching.

When I first came to the Unites States, a friend of mine took me to meet a group of businessmen. I was blessed to meet them because their business existed for one sole purpose, to generate income to support ministries. They donated their profit to support missions around the world. I pray that God will raise up more businesses like that.

We need to witness Jesus as the richest person in the universe. God said,

> "And you shall remember the Lord your God, for *it is* He who gives you *power to get wealth*, that He may establish His covenant which He swore to your fathers, as *it is* this day" (Deuteronomy 8:18).

The church needs to train believers to tap into that power of God to create wealth to establish God's covenant. God knows it takes serious wealth to establish His covenant, so He gave His power to His children to create it. But most of us are still asking God for free money. Do not ask God for free money; ask Him for the power to create wealth. God never gave free money to anyone in the Bible. He always gave an idea or instruction and showed people how to apply an idea or obey instructions. This process generated money that met their need.

One of the spiritual gifts Paul mentioned in Romans 12 is giving. How can we give if we do not have anything? In order to give, we need to have a way to generate money. This not only speaks about giving money, but about giving our time, love, kindness, forgiveness, and much more.

Don't try to copy someone else. Instead, find out how the power of the Holy Spirit wants to manifest through you to witness for Jesus. There are millions of ways to witness for Jesus. You can be a chef and witness for Jesus through the creativity of cooking. We are uniquely created with particular gifts and talents. Do not limit God and try to put Him in a box. Do not use the Holy Spirit only to prophesy, heal, and speak in tongues. They are a few of His gifts, but that's not the Person of the Holy Spirit. If I give you a car as a gift, that car is not me, the person; that is just one of my gifts. I have given many things as gifts to various people, especially my books, but none of those gifts represent my total being. It is very sad today that many know the Holy Spirit only for His gifts.

Ask the Holy Spirit to help you know Him and to discover your uniqueness; break off the mold that religion and culture have put upon you. *Be the only you who ever lived on the face of the earth.* There is only one David, Moses, and Esther in the Bible. The world has yet to see everything God intended for His church and through His church.

The Religious Spirit's Deception

The church operated as a kingdom and reigned until it was taken over by the religious spirit. The same thing happened to Israel in the Old Testament. Israel was a kingdom of priests. God wanted to bring His salvation to the ends of the earth through them. They rejected His call and kept the blessings to themselves. So Jesus said He would take the kingdom from them and give it to a nation that will bear its fruit.

> "Therefore I say to you, the kingdom of God will be taken from you and given to a nation bearing the fruits of it" (Matthew 21:43).

Which nation is Jesus talking about in the above verse? I believe the church is that nation. We are called a holy nation in 1 Peter 2:9. God gave His kingdom to the people of Israel but they did not fulfill His purpose so He took it from them and gave it to the church. Now it is our season. There is also a chance that the church will miss God's agenda because they are preoccupied with many other things than God's priority, which is reaching nations with the gospel of the kingdom.

Believers in the early church were taught and trained to reign as kings, as Adam did—not to sing. When the church was deceived and blinded by the religious spirit, we lost our influence and dominion and the devil took over the world system…again. Please read Paul's testimony about the Corinthian church.

> "You are already full! You are already rich! You have reigned as kings without us—and indeed I could wish

you did reign, that we also might reign with you!" (1 Corinthians 4:8).

Chapter 9

Kingdom Evangelism, Part 2

"Arise, O God, judge the earth; for You shall inherit all nations" (Psalm 82:8).

No nation on earth is closed to the gospel of the kingdom. Some nations are closed to the religious gospel we have been preaching, but everyone will press in to the kingdom when the kingdom of God is preached. When I say *preached*, I am not just talking about proclaiming in words, but by manifesting the kingdom through what we do because everyone needs the kingdom and everyone is looking for it.

> "The law and the prophets *were* until John. Since that time the kingdom of God has been preached, and everyone is pressing into it" (Luke 16:16).

How do we preach the gospel of the kingdom? We need to apply the wisdom of God to preach it. Every nation on earth is facing an enormous amount of problems. Light is the solution for darkness and we are the light of the world.

When the British came to India and other nations, they had the perfect opportunity to preach the gospel. They are supposedly Christians, but they only exploited those nations for economic gain. They even forbade missionaries from preaching and did not allow them to come to India. They missed a huge opportunity. The same is true in other countries. As we go to the places we are called, let us not make the same mistake.

In all the kingdom parables, Jesus used natural things to reveal a mystery of the kingdom. There is nothing wrong with us doing that today! Jesus was giving us a key, or a seed, to manifest the gospel of the kingdom: To use something in the natural: water, oil, education, product, food, business—anything and everything to *preach* the gospel of the kingdom!

Jesus used every aspect of our life and nation to explain to us the kingdom of God. He referred to the court system, construction, the army, the economy, agriculture, education, family, relationships, and every industry that is out there. What He is saying to us is that nothing is exempt from the reach of the gospel of the kingdom. He was not against nations fighting each other. He even said that when a king goes to fight against another, he has to calculate the cost and how many there are against him.

> "Or what king, going to make war against another king, does not sit down first and consider whether he is able with ten thousand to meet him who comes against him with twenty thousand? Or else, while the other is still a great way off, he sends a delegation and asks conditions of peace" (Luke 14:31-32).

He talked about construction and the housing industry.

> "For which of you, intending to build a tower, does not sit down first and count the cost, whether he has *enough* to finish *it*— lest, after he has laid the foundation, and is not able to finish, all who see *it* begin to mock him, saying, 'This man began to build and was not able to finish'?" (Luke 14:28-30).

> "Therefore whoever hears these sayings of Mine, and does them, I will liken him to a wise man who built his house on the rock" (Matthew 7:24).

Jesus used food, agriculture, precious metals, water, and different products like wine, garments, land, water, sea, fish, farming, money, and pearls to preach the gospel. We can use the same, not to tell stories with them, but to do it in real life and show the world our God.

No government on earth will say no to a company or organization that is willing to solve a problem for them. But they will say no if you ask for permission to conduct a crusade. Crusades will never save a nation. We are looking for restoration and transformation of nations.

The Catholics went into countries and solved educational and medical problems. They established schools and hospitals in almost every nation under heaven. Therefore they found a place in society and gained influence.

Jesus came to solve a problem, the sin problem. Likewise, each of us is sent here to solve a problem. When you solve a problem you will gain influence, and it will open the door wide and free. Daniel and Joseph solved national problems and they changed nations. That is kingdom evangelism. If the church would become less religious and more kingdom-minded, this world would be a better place in no time!

Unemployment is a huge problem in many countries. If you start a company and create job opportunities for people, it will give you favor and open doors. No one will be able to prevent you from going into any nation.

Harvesting the Fields

> "Then He said to His disciples, "The harvest truly *is* plentiful, but the laborers *are* few" (Matthew 9:37).

How do we harvest the world, and what kind of tools will we use? God uses a different method for harvesting nations. He used Joseph to harvest the economy, agriculture, and the land of Egypt. As a result, the entire nation of Egypt was *reached*. In many nations their economy is ripe for harvest. By harvesting a system, you are harvesting an entire people who are connected to that system.

> "Do you not say, 'There are still four months and *then* comes the harvest'? Behold, I say to you, lift up your eyes and look at the fields, for they are already white for harvest!" (John 4:35).

In this verse Jesus is talking about fields. I thought by saying *field*, Jesus meant souls. Not necessarily. What kind of field is He talking about? There are different kinds of fields. In another parable He said, "…the field is the world" (Matthew 13:38a). Jesus knew then how twenty-first century people would communicate. It is common today that when people talk about their profession they use terms like "medical field," "IT field," "fashion field," and so on. What they mean by it is they are doing a job that is connected to medicine, technology, or fashion; they are the different fields of this world. Jesus is saying those fields are ripe for harvest. That means when we administer God's kingdom by starting various enterprises in those fields, people who are connected or working in them will be reached with the gospel of the kingdom.

The reason we are not able to reach nations today is because we do not understand the fields to which people are connected, neither do we know how to harvest those fields. We do not train or equip believers with that mindset. We have more preachers and Bible schools that produce preachers than at any other time in history. Even in Jesus's time there were plenty of religious workers. By saying the laborers are few He does not mean we have less ministers. He is talking with a kingdom mindset.

In many nations the agricultural field is ripe for harvest. That means there is opportunity for believers to come up with creative ideas and solutions for good food production to meet the needs of the people and alleviate hunger and food-related sicknesses. When you do that, you are influencing that nation and harvesting souls that are connected to that field.

The education fields are ripe for harvest. Schools do not teach what is required for children to learn in life. They teach all kinds of stuff that we will never use, and do not teach us what is essential to life. We need to totally transform the field of education and bring kingdom education.

When you go fishing, you either take a net or a hook depending on where you are going to fish; you need the appropriate equipment. When we harvest the land, we use the proper tools too. When we fish for men, as Jesus told His disciples, what kind of equipment should we use? How do we fish for men?

Economy, agriculture, education, and media are just "nets" to fish for men and women. People are connected to those components and they cannot live without them. We need to receive from God the wisdom to harvest those souls.

There are a number of people we can win through healing and miracles, but everyone on earth is not sick in their body or aware of their need. We must use the appropriate tools for each people group. When we use all the existing tools to harvest all of the fields, then we will reach the entire nation with the gospel of the kingdom. It's not going to happen just through crusades and personal evangelism.

Jesus said in Matthew 13:47-48, "Again, the kingdom of heaven is like a dragnet that was cast into the sea and gathered some of every kind, which, when it was full, they drew to shore; and they sat down and gathered the good into vessels, but threw the bad away."

To explain the mysteries of the kingdom of heaven, Jesus used fishing as an example. In the above parable, the kingdom of heaven is the dragnet. The sea is the world. The person casting the net is God. The good are sons of the kingdom and the bad are the children of the wicked one. For each field, we need to use a different kind of dragnet. To harvest people who are connected to economy, we need to use an economic dragnet. There are many dragnets in the kingdom of God.

The reason Jesus sent His disciples out to only heal and cast out demons is because the kingdom of God had not yet fully come at that time. It came on the Day of Pentecost with the coming of the Holy Spirit. Kingdom evangelism began on that day. On that first day, people from every nation heard and witnessed the arrival of the Holy Spirit.

Reaching the World

John 3:16 is one of the most famous and misinterpreted verses in the Bible. I always wondered why the Bible says God so loved the world. What does God have to do with the world? Why didn't He just say God so loved the people, or humans? The Greek word for "world" is *cosmos*. John 3:17 is as important as John 3:16.

> "For God did not send His Son into the world to condemn the world, but that the world through Him might be saved" (John 3:17).

There are two very important things to understand from these verses. The first is that God loves this world very much and the second is that He wanted to save it. The people He put in this world to do that have been trying to escape the world for the last two thousand years, or waiting for it to end. John 3:17 tells us the reason God so loved the world. *God sent His Son not to end this world but to save it.* Instead of partnering with God to save it they were waiting for it to be destroyed. We have only been trying to save the people and not the world.

Jesus said, "As You sent Me into the world, I also have sent them into the world" (John 17:18).[77]

We are not *of* this world but we have been sent into this world, just like the Father sent Jesus. As long as Jesus was in this world He was the

---

77 See John 20:21.

light of this world; since He left we became the light and solution to the problems of this world.[78]

That is why Jesus prayed to His Father in John 17, not to take us out of this world, but to keep us right here until we finish the job He gave us to do.

> "I do not pray that You should take them out of the world, but that You should keep them from the evil one" (John 17:15).

When you save the world, the people in it will be saved as well. The question is: What is the world? The world is a system in which a person or a thing lives. For a banker, the economy is his world. For a musician, music is his world.

For a fish, the water or the ocean is its world. If a fish lives in contaminated water, that water is slowly killing it, even though the fish may not realize it. You have a burden to save that fish. To save a fish you do not take the fish out of the water. If you do, it will die. If you want to save a fish, you save the water (its world), and then the fish will be saved.

That is what we have been doing for so long. We have been trying to save people by taking them out of the world. It has not been effective, and they are dying without fulfilling their purpose. As a result, this world is dying as well when God wants to use us to reach and save the world.

For a bird, the air is its world. For an animal, the jungle is its world. What is the world for humans? The economy is part of our world; we cannot live without it. Education is part of our world. Agriculture is part of our world. We cannot live without food. Each human being is connected to one or more of those seven components of which the world system consists. They are culture; religion; government; economy; education; media and entertainment; and science and technology. When you reach one of those "worlds" with the gospel of the kingdom, you will win every

---

78 See John 9:5 and Matthew 5:14.

soul that is connected to that component. They all are ripe for harvest in every nation. When we harvest these *fields* we will see the largest ingathering of souls coming into the kingdom of God.

Why Jesus Died for Us

As just stated, we are very familiar with John 3:16, but not John 3:17. There is a difference between the Earth and the world. The Earth is the physical planet and the world is the system by which Earth and everything in it functions. In technical terms, Earth is the hardware and the world is the software by which it operates. The world and the kingdom of God are two different operating systems and both operate according to principles that oppose each other. Both are trying to work through the world to reach humans because every human being is connected to the world. We cannot live without it. They are like water and oil; no matter how much we try, they will not mix.

God has been trying to save the world because it is His creation and it belongs to Him. When the Bible uses the word *world* it has different meanings.

> "He was in the world, and the world was made through Him, and the world did not know Him" (John 1:10).

> "God, who at various times and in various ways spoke in time past to the fathers by the prophets, has in these last days spoken to us by *His* Son, whom He has appointed heir of all things, through whom also He made the worlds" (Hebrews 1:1-2).

> "For *God so loved the world* that He gave His only begotten Son, that whoever believes in Him should not perish but have everlasting life" (John 3:16).

I used to believe that when God said He loved the world it meant He loved human beings, because that is what everyone preached. If He loved only human beings, He would have said, "God so loved humanity (or people) that He gave His only begotten Son." God never wastes a word or uses a word just for fun, like we do sometimes. The word "world" here means more than just humans. We are just one of the species that lives in this world.

Jesus also said He is the light of this world.[79] Very few understand the relationship and the love God has for this world and what He has been trying to do in and through it.

As I mentioned above, God knew that if He saved the world, it would automatically save humanity because we live in the world and cannot live without it. When it says, "God so loved the world," it is talking about the system by which this earth operates and the people who are connected to it. The devil illegally took over this world and became the god of this world. Actually, he stole that from us.

When the Bible says the devil is the god of this world, it does not mean he is our god, but the god of the system by which this earth operates. People are trapped in it and he controls them through it.

> "Whose minds the god of this age has blinded, who do not believe, lest the light of the gospel of the glory of Christ, who is the image of God, should shine on them" (2 Corinthians 4:4).

The Bible also says that we should not love the world or the things in it. The word "world" in this verse cannot mean people because we are supposed to love people. The same Greek word is used in John 3:16 and 1 John 2:15. The question arises: Why would God love the world so much but tell us not to love it? God saw the hidden danger posed for us if we love the world because of the influence the devil has over the world system at the present time. The devil will use this world and all its allurements

---

79 See John 8:12 and 9:5.

to draw us in and deviate us from our kingdom purpose, the area we are supposed to reclaim. God knows it is easy for us to get blinded by the enemy if we love the world.

That is what the devil tried to do to Jesus when he tempted Him. He offered Him this world, its kingdoms, and their glory. The devil knew that Jesus is the owner and the legal heir of this world, but the world had been delivered to the devil by man, and Jesus had come to take it back from him. He was offering it to Jesus through a shortcut,[80] without going to the cross. Thank God Jesus did not accept his offer.

> "Do not love the world or the things in the world. If anyone loves the world, the love of the Father is not in him" (1 John 2:15).

> "We know that we are children of God and that the world around us is under the control of the evil one" (1 John 5:19 NLT).

> "So don't be surprised, dear brothers and sisters, if the world hates you" (1 John 3:13 NLT).

The Ruler of This World Has Already Been Judged

Jesus judged the ruler of this world, Satan, two thousand years ago, but Satan is still acting as if he owns the world because the people God put on earth do not understand that it is finished. They are still waiting for some future event.

> "Of judgment, because *the ruler of this world* is judged" (John 16:11).

This verse is talking about an event that already occurred.

---

[80] See Matthew 4:8-10 and Luke 4:5-8.

Satan is also known as the prince of the power of the air. We read in Ephesians 2:2, "In which you once walked according to the course of this world, according to the *prince of the power of the air,* the *spirit* who now works in the sons of disobedience."

He is also known as the ruler of this world. "Now is the judgment of this world; now the ruler of this world will be cast out" (John 12:31).

Please note the word "now" in this verse. Jesus did not say two thousand years from now the judgment of this world will happen, or on the final Judgment Day, or after His second coming. He said, "Now," which means more than two thousand years ago this world was judged and the ruler of it was cast out. There are not very many people who act like they believe this truth.

Jesus called him the ruler of this world. "I will no longer talk much with you, for the ruler of this world is coming, and he has nothing in Me" (John 14:30).

"Rulers of the darkness of this *age*..." (Ephesians 6:12)

According to the above verses, Jesus judged the world and the prince (or the god) of it, and cast him out of his domain. Now the world belongs to us, and most of us do not even know it. As Paul writes in 1 Corinthians 3:21-23:

> "Therefore let no one boast in men. For all things are yours: whether Paul or Apollos or Cephas, or the world or life or death, or things present or things to come—all are yours. And you *are* Christ's, and Christ *is* God's."

The enemy does not want to admit defeat. God knows that the only people who can save this world for Him is us, so He gave His life for us that we can be redeemed and, in turn, turn around and restore the world for Him. Unfortunately we have been singing for so long that this world isn't our home and we are going to fly away, that we have forgotten our mission, if we ever understood it in the first place. That is what the religious spirit does to us. The church can easily win this world for King Jesus in no time at all, but we need to believe the Bible and act on it if that is to happen.

Children Who Reign

God made Abraham and his seed the heirs of this world (Romans 4:13). We are Abraham's seed through faith in Jesus Christ (Galatians 3:29). We are supposed to be ruling and reigning as God's children right now here on earth. That is what Abraham and his seed did in the Old Testament.

Most believers think this world and its kingdom will be destroyed, but that is not what the Bible says. It says the opposite. Jesus is waiting for this world and its kingdoms to be His to rule and reign forever. In Revelation, we read that when the seventh angel sounds the trumpet that is exactly what is going to happen.

> "Then the seventh angel sounded: And there were loud voices in heaven, saying, "The kingdoms of this world have become *the kingdoms* of our Lord and of His Christ, and He shall reign forever and ever!" (Revelation 11:15).

Prayer

Dear heavenly Father, thank You so much for giving me Your kingdom and creating me as a king or queen on this earth. Open my eyes to see and my heart to receive the mysteries of Your kingdom. Deliver me from the influence of the religious spirit. Please make me part of what You are doing on this earth right now. I dedicate my life and everything I have to establishing Your kingdom and for Your purpose, to see Your will be done on earth as it is in heaven. In Jesus Christ's holy name I pray. Amen.

As you read this book, please ask the Father for *your* nation and other nations that you are passionate about as an inheritance for Jesus Christ our King and for His kingdom.

I believe this book has been a blessing to you. Please use it for Bible study groups. If you want to order more copies, just let us know. I could only mention here a fraction of the revelation God gave me about His kingdom. If you want to know more about His kingdom, please make sure to get parts 1, 2, and 3 of the Kingdom Awareness Series: *The Power and Authority of the Church: Equipping the Saints to Administer God's Kingdom on Earth (Volume 1), Kingdom Secrets to Worry Free Living (Volume 2), and Releasing Kings and Queens to Their Original Intent (Volume 3).*

I strongly recommend that you obtain more copies of this book and do a group Bible study in your church, ministry or home. Learn and apply the principles revealed in it and be a part of what God is doing right now on the earth!

If you would like to have Abraham John come and speak at your church, small groups, or conference, please contact us to know more about his itinerary.

To order more copies of this book and other resources please contact:

Maximum Impact Ministries
Phone: 1(800) 558 5020
email: mim@maximpact.org
www.TheKingdomNetwork.org

More Books & Resources

DISCIPLING NATIONS SERIES

Kingdom Mandate (for any donation)
Discovering the Lost Kingdom (Volume 1) $14.00
Purpose, Calling, and Gifts (Volume 2) $15.00
God's Original Design (Volume 3) $20.00
Seeing, Entering, and Manifesting the Kingdom of God (Volume 4)$20.00
The Ekklesia (Volume 5) $30.00
The Gospel of the Kingdom (Volume 6) $20.00
Power and Authority of the Church (Volume 7) $15.00
Kingdom Family (Volume 8) $15.00
The Birthing of a Kingdom Nation (Volume 9) $20.00
What Happened to God? (Volume10) $20.00
7 Dimensions and Operations of the Kingdom of God (Volume 11) $15.00
Kingdom Economy (Volume 12) $15.00
Kingdom Government (Volume 13) $15.00
Releasing Kings and Queens to their Original Intent (Volume 14) $10.00
Kingdom Secrets to Restoring Nations Back to God (Volume 15) $20.00
Keys to Fulfilling Your Kingdom Assignment (Volume 16) $15.00

KINGDOM LIVING SERIES

The Three Most Important Decisions of Your Life $15.00
Recognizing God's Timing for Your Life $12.00
Overcoming the Spirit of Poverty $10.00
Seven Kinds of Believers $10.00
7 Dimensions of God's Glory $5.00
7 Dimensions of God's Grace $10.00
7 Kinds of Faith $7.00

HEALING OF THE NATIONS SERIES

Principles of Self Governance $20.00

KINGDOM BOOKS FOR KIDS

Genesis 126 Three Volume Book set for boys $25.00
Genesis 126 Three Volume Book set for boys $25.00

Genesis 126 Coloring Books for Boys $15.00
Genesis 126 Coloring Books for Girls $15.00

GENESIS 126 TEACHER'S MANUAL

Level 1 6-8 years $15.00
Level 2 8-10 years $15.00
Level 3 10-12 years $15.00

TO PLACE AN ORDER:

www.TheKingdomNetwork.org
Phone: 1-800-558-5020
Email: info@TheKingdomNetwork.org

Are you struggling to discover your **PURPOSE ?**
You are not supposed to fit in but stand out !

Sign up today for the
FREE Online Kingdom Course

DISCOVERING

THE LOST KINGDOM

In this course you'll DISCOVER:

>> Your true identity and purpose
>> What God is doing on the earth and how you can partner with Him in it
>> Why God created the earth and put us on this planet
>> And much more ...

Why are people becoming more and more disinterested in **church and religion** globally?
Join the course, and discover
what your soul has been searching for all along.

FREE BOOK AND STUDY GUIDE

Other courses available
>> DISCOVERING PURPOSE, CALLING AND GIFTS
>> SEEING, ENTERING AND MANIFESTING THE KINGDOM
>> GOD'S ORIGINAL DESIGN
>> The Ekklesia
>> The Next move of GOD
   And more ...

Register Now @ **www.TheKingdomUniversity.org**

Welcome to
KINGDOM DELIVERANCE
— WORKSHOP —

Are you tired of waiting and looking for breakthroughs? Kingdom of God has the answer.

This kingdom deconstruct workshop is divided into EIGHT major categories which deal with the eight major areas of our life. Each one is connected to the next, and so if one of these areas dysfunctions, it will affect all other areas of your life.

1. Relationship with the Father
2. Spiritual Healing
3. Emotional Healing
4. Recognizing Purpose and Calling
5. Identifying and Mastering Natural and Spiritual Gifts
6. Finances—Learning to Live in Kingdom Economy
7. Healing Relationships
8. Physical Health

Take action now. Order all 8 workshop manuals today !

Thank you so much for taking the courses from The Kingdom University. Taking a course is only the first step. We are pleased to present you with the next step—that of going through the process to get rid of all the extra weights that have been slowing and hindering you from fully living out your kingdom assignment.

Call 1 800 558 5020   www.TheKingdomNetwork.org